Our Debt to Greece and Rome

EDITORS
GEORGE DEPUE HADZSITS, PH.D.

DAVID MOORE ROBINSON, PH.D., LL.D.

PSYCHOLOGY
ANCIENT AND MODERN

BY

GEORGE SIDNEY BRETT, M.A. (Oxon.)

COOPER SQUARE PUBLISHERS, INC.

NEW YORK

1963

Published 1963 by Cooper Square Publishers, Inc.
59 Fourth Avenue, New York 3, N. Y.
Library of Congress Catalog Card No. 63-10293

PREFACE

IN modern times the word psychology has come to have a new meaning. It was first used in the sixteenth century in a way that was nearly equivalent to the Latin phrase " de anima." For a time the word pneumatology was preferred, but finally psychology became the common title for all works that dealt with the functions of the soul. With the progress of biology the word has taken on a different meaning and is no longer to be regarded as implying any reference to a soul but merely as indicating the scientific study of a certain class of phenomena.

The older works on classical psychology were influenced by the attitude of the times to which they belonged. Emphasis was laid on the more speculative and metaphysical aspects of the texts and this led to the general idea that the classical writers no longer had any message for the modern reader. Recently interest has revived along different lines. The historian of

science, approaching the ancient writers from
an angle not usually selected by classical scholars, has discovered and revealed an unsus-
pected wealth of material. In particular the
subject of psychology has benefited by this
movement. It seems to have remained too long
under the shadow of that condemnation which
fell upon the degenerate Aristotelians who
made themselves ridiculous in the days of Galileo. Now that we can see more clearly how far
those Aristotelians were removed from the
spirit of the real classical age and how fresh
and natural the original outlook had been, it is
time to review the whole question again.

The reader is asked to take these remarks as
an explanation of the point of view from which
psychology has been treated in the following
pages. It may occur to some that the traditional topics should have been discussed more
completely and that more space should have
been given to such matters as the proofs of immortality, pure pleasures, and the like. But
subjects of this kind are inevitably included
in the general accounts of ancient philosophy
and with the small space at the disposal of the
writer it seemed desirable to concentrate on the
material which shows how the classical writers

really laid the foundation for work that has since been done in the recognized branches of psychology. It is in fact the middle part of the subject which most repays study today. The Greeks in particular took so direct and simple a view of life and organic functions that it seems as if the intervening centuries had melted away and the men of the nineteenth century were taking up the work just as it was left in the last days of Athens and Alexandria. There is no theory more characteristic of modern psychology than the theory of emotions as irrational drives made potent by the depth of their foundations in the most primitive or " vegetative " part of the psychophysical organism. Yet this is the view we find writ large through the works of Plato and Aristotle. Many other examples will be found in the account given in these pages, but the whole matter can be summed up in the statement that the original point of view, lost somewhere in transit, was essentially biological.

This fact, however, would not justify a wholesale reproduction of all that passed for science among the Greeks or their successors in the Roman world. Accordingly no attempt has been made to include the details of sense-physiology. To do so would be to expend time and space on what is essentially antiquated. If, in consequence, the description of ancient psychology should seem to be unfair and to provide no basis for appreciating its defects, the only defence that can be offered is that the error is on the right side. Students of the classics today require to cultivate an appreciation of the really great amount of valuable material which they can find in their authors if they know how to look for it and how to estimate it. To do this properly requires some acquaintance with modern work in the same fields. The object which has been kept in view in constructing this sketch of ancient psychology is to show the reader how to connect the wisdom of the classical writers with the more elaborate and technical work which has slowly grown from those small beginnings.

CONTENTS

CONTENTS

PSYCHOLOGY,
ANCIENT AND MODERN

PSYCHOLOGY
ANCIENT AND MODERN

PSYCHOLOGY, ANCIENT AND MODERN

I. GENERAL PSYCHOLOGY

1. THE PHYSIOLOGICAL BASIS

IN this twentieth century of our era, psychology claims to be a science and, in spite of some opposition, may be judged to have established that claim. The reason for now making this claim in a rather emphatic manner is to be found in the complete tradition which has for centuries excluded the soul from the field of the sciences. The point of view established most effectively by Descartes was actually an old tradition to which Descartes gave a new lease of life. According to this tradition there is a mysterious difference between soul and body; they are distinct " essences "; nothing that is true of the one will be true of the other; especially because the soul is " unextended " and therefore no method involving quantity or measurement can be applied to it.

Such was the traditional doctrine and it may be traced back at least as far at St. Augustine (A.D. 430). Most people would think at once of Plato and assert that the tradition began in Plato's works, but that is a point to be considered with more leisure. For practical purposes it is the influence on European thought of Jewish and Christian creeds which must be held accountable for the subsequent mixture of theories. The religious interest begins from the consideration of the moral life, the estimation of values, and then constructs a world of values in which the immortal soul experiences to the full either the penalties of evil doing or the rewards of virtue. But before this transcendent life can begin there must be a period of time spent on the earth. Heaven may be more important but earth is nearer; and for every individual who feels the significance of eternity there will be ten who are wholly interested in works and days. So we find a rift in the doctrine, as simple and as natural as anything could be. For by his own act of thought man has constituted himself a creature poised between time and eternity. He looks

[4]

down in the slime of the pit whence he was digged, sees there the animals and says " But for the grace of God there go I." He looks up to the vault of heaven and in looking aspires to that transcendent realm of order, peace, and beauty, feeling a conviction of mystical union between " the starry heavens above and the moral law within."

If we use the term psychology in the usual loose manner to indicate all that may be said about the soul, we shall be met from the very beginning with this ambiguity of meaning. The modern claim that psychology shall be scientific means primarily that all speculative elements, whether rightly called religious or moral or theological or spiritual, shall be excluded entirely from the field of enquiry. If by so doing one half of the subject is eliminated, then the modern psychologist is contented to take no more than his half. When the supernatural is thus cut out, there remains the natural, and the consequent doctrine may be called the naturalistic doctrine of the psychic organism. This is virtually the standpoint of modern psychology, and it is of great importance to notice that in this point the method of psychology becomes distinctively the method of Aristotle. In the

[5]

twenty-two hundred years that have elapsed since the death of Aristotle, the science of the soul has never been nearer the Aristotelian ideas than it is today. The evidence for this assertion must be found first of all in a statement of the Greek doctrine of the soul, and then in the history of the tradition through the stages of its transit from ancient to modern times.

When the modern psychologist becomes interested in the history of his science he usually goes back to Aristotle, regarding his work as the sum and substance of Greek achievements in this field. This view is not devoid of justification, for Aristotle's work is unequalled for either quality or precision or actual historical influence. But the scholar who looks at a science from the standpoint of humanism and is interested in its development as a phase of national life, will not be satisfied with such a limited estimate of the subject. On the contrary he will recollect that Aristotle stood at the very end of the classical Greek development and was himself a diligent student of his predecessors, owing much of his completeness and finality to the fact that he was able to incorporate in his work all that seemed to him valuable

in the earlier schools of thought. Considering
the time at which he lived, Aristotle had unique
opportunities for doing justice to the problem of
the soul. The decay of primitive tribal religions for a brief time cleared away many
dogmas and superstitions. By birth and training Aristotle was more equipped for scientific
enquiry than for religious or theological speculation. The fact that his father was a physician at the court of the Macedonian ruler
Amyntas is important for two reasons: it explains Aristotle's tendency to ignore the Greek
religious dogmas and his obvious bias toward
a pure science of the organism. On the other
hand, Aristotle is in the full sense of the term a
philosopher. As he will not venture into the
region of speculation even so far as Plato went,
so he refuses with equal obstinacy to adopt any
purely materialistic or mechanical theory by
which life and mind could be reduced to motion
and atoms. By his power of combining medical and philosophical methods Aristotle became
something equivalent to the modern biologist,
though it is necessary to remember that the ad-
jectives medical and biological are not to be
used without due reference to the changes
which they have undergone as those sciences

[7]

developed. It is enough for the present to say that in Aristotle's case these words really mean that his standpoint was determined by his idea of living organisms and their functions.

In the fifth century before Christ the science of animal organisms was the product mainly of the medical practice and the theories which partly controlled and partly emerged from that practice. The major part of this has been preserved in the so-called Hippocratic writings and it will be necessary first to consider what parts of these writings are connected with the idea of a soul.

When we attempt to estimate our debt to the Greeks and Romans it is necessary to keep in mind the exact points at which it is possible to declare with honesty that any actual debt exists. As the subject to be valued is in this case psychology, and whatever exists today as psychology must be classified among the sciences, the points worthy of consideration must be those which form a permanent element in the evolution of this science. On this principle it will be unnecessary to review all the curious details which are properly assigned to religion and anthropology. It may be taken for granted that the primitive inhabitants of the Greek peninsula enjoyed and communicated the experiences common to all known branches of the human family. They dreamed dreams; they saw ghosts; they looked with awe on the mysterious phenomena of intoxication, inspiration, or epilepsy; they saw the red blood flow as life ebbed from the wounded body; they knew how pale and motionless the corpse lies on its bier. In Homer we find all these things recorded with the naive simplicity of the earliest traditions, but psychology as a science owes no real debt to such records.

Parallel with these early records of common observations we find the first traces of speculation about the continuation of life after death. In all the primitive beliefs recorded by anthropologists there are traces of beliefs about some form of existence after the individual ceases to live among his companions. It may be that he goes down into Sheol as the Hebrews thought, or descends into Hades as the Homeric heroes do, or that some special element is released from the body to stand before the judgment throne of a deity hereafter, as the Persians and Egyptians believed. But these matters belong to the history of religions and though in some ways historical psychology is affected by the desire to retain within its limits some elements that do not coincide with or perish with the material body, the movement of scientific thought is away from these speculations and, as our concern is primarily with the growth of a scientific psychology, they can be ignored without further excuse.

As compared with Babylonians, Persians, or Egyptians the Greeks seem to have had a peculiar gift for the kind of thinking which is strictly scientific. Beginning from a common basis of mythology the Greeks developed a scientific view of nature which rapidly surpassed the achievements of other peoples. Out of cosmogony they created cosmology; out of astrology they made astronomy; out of crude practical methods of measurement they made geometry; and out of human experience they constructed principles of order which were the beginnings of a complete science of Nature. The process was in one sense rapid, yet at the same time slow in as much as false ideas were abundant, true ideas few and immature, instruments imperfect and rare. The Greeks triumphed in the end because their leaders had the right idea of scientific method. Their concept of nature was dominated by the simple ideas of

Being and Becoming. Instead of multiplying theories about creation they began to look for the actual origin and development of individual things, and this was in itself a priceless contribution to intellectual progress. It alone accounts for the fact that the modern world looks back to the Greeks as the real fathers of modern science.

" Nature " is an ambiguous word and the Greek term φύσις, " Physis," was equally ambiguous. It survives today in the two scientific terms " physics " and " physiology," and these represent the primary divisions of that subject which the early Greek thinkers would have called "physics." Until very recent times physics was included in the subject called " natural philosophy," a term which is even nearer the standpoint of the Greeks. For philosophy was originally a name for all enquiries by which men strove to satisfy the pure desire for knowledge, as distinct from the technical arts which seemed to satisfy the demand for things that could be made and used. We find accordingly that the Greek tradition begins with the study of nature as a whole and by degrees maps out distinct parts of this field until in the later Alexandrian period a form of specialization appears, the separate sciences have distinct names and men devote themselves exclusively to one or the other branch of knowledge.

Evolution manifests itself in the sciences as it does elsewhere. In the beginning " all things were together," but in the process of time a separation is achieved, the undifferentiated becomes distinct, and chaos is reduced to order. This is not the effect of any conscious purpose. It is rather an immanent process of growth by which the mass of material increases until it breaks up into distinct parts, with only the unity that is constituted by more or less relationship between the parts. Critics who lack imagination condemn the early Greek philosophers for trying to solve first the problem of the Universe. But if we cannot " indict a nation," it is still more certain that we cannot indict humanity. History cannot be criticized in this way, and if it could, there would be good reason for thinking this criticism essentially false. For the method thus unconsciously pursued had the important result of discovering slowly and surely man's place in nature. The most significant point in this result is the consequent grasp of the relation which every organism has to its environment and of the fact that nature must be treated as a class of objects in which there are many smaller classes. The cosmos includes the two great classes of inanimate and animate objects; the animate objects include plants, animals, and men; if to this we add the remark that "animate" means "besouled," the significance of this approach to the subject will be manifest. The comprehensiveness of the outlook secures a fair treatment of all the phenomena without premature bias toward either a narrow materialism or a dogmatic spiritualism.

Psychology as it appears in the classical Greek times is a body of doctrine which gradually emerges from cosmology by way of a broad physiological doctrine of vital functions and a more limited consideration of animal and human activities. Consequently the progress toward the special doctrine of the soul must be traced through these stages in order to obtain an exact idea of the nature and value of the results. While the terms cannot, at this stage, be regarded as very exact we may refer to the whole movement as the development of Greek medicine in so far as that was a science of the organism and not an art of healing.

With a suddenness which is rather startling

we find a physician in the sixth century before Christ asserting a definite connection between the brain and conscious life. Alkmaeon of Crotona (550–500 B.C.) is credited with making dissections, asserting that the brain is the organ of mind, discovering the " optic nerve " and explaining the acts of vision and hearing. It is impossible to say how much of this is true, while it is certain that the terms cannot be taken very seriously. But the tradition may be accepted as indicating that in the Pythagorean schools of the sixth century some work was done which deserves to be recorded as the real beginning of a physiology of the senses.

The exact definition of psychology is still a matter for dispute. Some writers prefer to regard psychology as " pure " and they omit all reference to anatomy or physiology; others take the opposite extreme, attempting to explain all kinds of behavior as dependent on the physiology of nerve, muscle, and gland; a third class adopts the principle of judicious selection and practices the doctrine of the golden mean. This last class is truly Greek in more than one sense: it not only follows the rule which became a catchword among Greek moralists, but it also perpetuates that form of psychology which we may regard as the genuine Greek type. For this class of psychologists it is axiomatically true that psychology comprises first an account of the nerves, then a description of the functions which can be localized, and finally an introspective account of such activities as belief or apperceptions about which the question of localization is either irrelevant or impossible. It is not necessary to discuss the relative merits of these theories of method; it is enough to recognize that the last is really equivalent to the process by which psychology came into being historically and that the Greek writers built by slow accumulation that mass of physiological and non-physiological observations which finally appears as the " science of the soul." To define this science adequately it is therefore necessary to show what equipment the Greeks had for describing the structure and functions of the organism. It is necessary, in other words, to present in proper order, first, the idea of the psychophysical organism, then, the doctrine of sense perception, and, finally, the mechanism of the mind in its main operations of knowing and willing.

Alkmaeon has been cited as probably the first Greek anatomist. This term must be taken in a very wide sense, for it is certain that in the sixth century before Christ there was very little knowledge about the body and very little organized investigation. The science of the body, whether human or animal, was in a state of transition. Primitive art and, still more, the mature Greek art shows a wonderful sense for external form and surface anatomy. But knowledge of the inward parts began at first from chance observations, such as might occur from seeing deep wounds, or from the organized but unscientific " inspection " of entrails by augurs and soothsayers. The results of this early period amounted to nothing but crude facts: the existence of the bones, entrails, spleen, liver, heart, lungs, trachea, and " brain " was thus discovered; but in the case of the " brain " it is well to remember that it was known only as " the contents of the skull," the " encephalon," and not as the complex structure described by later anatomists.

Similar crude observations account for the very natural belief that the organ of vision is the eye, the organ of hearing the ear, and of smell the nose; the remainder of the traditional

five senses, taste and touch, were not so easy
to determine though it was easy to guess that
taste was due to some fluids in the mouth and
that touch was a function of the skin at any
part of the body. As this is not a history of
anatomy or physiology we need not recount all
the details of the various theories which are to
be found in recorded sayings of the Greek
" physical " philosophers.[1] The real interest of
this period is not in the solutions but in the discovery of the problem of sense affection. What
the Greeks of this age really achieved was the
formulation of the idea that in sensation there
is some effect produced inside the body by an
agent which is outside and must therefore have
some means of penetrating to the inward parts.
This step was important: it definitely created the
problem which we still designate as the problem
of the relation between stimulus and sensation.
The solutions offered were ingenious but for
various reasons they have no value as positive
results. It is a matter for perpetual wonder that
the Greek thinkers could develop a problem
and a method at a time when the available data
made correct solutions impossible. To suggest
the right problem and view it from the right
point of view is a mark of genius and also the

greatest contribution that any one person or century can bequeath to subsequent generations. As Francis Bacon rightly declared, the sciences should pass from inventor to improver, and accordingly all positive results should lead to better results and become obsolete by virtue of their own growth. Only dogmatism can persist unchanged, like an Egyptian mummy; the living body of knowledge must perpetually change just because it has vitality.

Regarding man as a creature immersed in the stream of cosmic events, the Greeks rightly guessed that the fundamental problem is to explain how the outer world produces the inner perception of that world. Unfortunately neither the anatomy nor the physiology was adequate to afford a correct explanation. The procedure accordingly becomes a mixture of logical hypotheses and apparent verifications. If the agent passes from the outside to the inside, there must be passages along which it travels. These are called the "paths" or "pores" (πόροι). The whole body is conceived as an object bombarded from without by particles of matter which vary in size and shape. There is a corresponding variation in the size of the pores and the different organs act like sieves, allowing the particles to pass through according to the due proportions between the sizes of the particles and the apertures. The plausibility of one science depends largely on its conformity with the results of another science, and this type of explanation coincided with the evolution of another great triumph of Greek physical speculation, the doctrine of atoms. Combining the atomic view of matter with the hypothesis of sense-organs as tube-like pathways leading inwards to the seat of sensation, the Greeks formulated a hypothetical science for the explanation of sense effects. The result is an astonishing product. In form it is complete and adequate; in detail untrue and useless. The form persists to the present day, for with greater refinement of terms we are still studying the transmission of the stimulus from the periphery to the central seat of sensation; the detail has been superseded by totally different ideas about the nature of the sense-organs and some of these ideas were developed by the Greeks themselves at a later stage.

The first and most obvious defect of the early theories is the total ignorance of the existence of nerves. The original word " neuron " could be used for any cord-like structure which was extended along a part of the body, and it was in fact a term which covered all such anatomical parts as sinews, tendons, and ligaments. As these were solid they allowed no passage for the incoming particles, and it was necessary to suppose that the sense-organs were more like veins or arteries. After a time the arteries were actually brought into the scheme, as we shall see. Plato and Aristotle constructed their elaborate psychological doctrines before the nerves were discovered.[2] The Alexandrian schools of medicine seem to have been the first to make sufficient study of anatomy to discover such obscure things as nerves. Herophilus (355–280 B.C.) and Erasistratus (330–250 B.C.) have the credit of first definitely tracing the course of some of the nerves, limiting the functions of sensation to the nerves, and so finally demonstrating the importance of the brain for intelligence. This is the most important contribution which the ancient medical schools made to the study of sensation, and it remained the high-water mark of achievement until the nineteenth century. The final form of the doctrine was due to Galen (A.D. 200) and as " Galenism " it remained, undisputed and unimproved, until the days of Leonardo da Vinci (A.D. 1527) and Vesalius (A.D. 1543).

The modern reader stands aghast at the idea of a psychology constructed without so much as an idea that the body contains nerves. Yet it remains true that the greatest contribution to psychology, Aristotle's treatise on the soul, preceded the work of the Alexandrian school. This fact raises some interesting problems. Is it after all necessary to know what it is in us that thinks and feels and wills? Do we yet know, or is the whole physiological machinery merely a collateral mass of information which we try to match point by point with our immediate knowledge of sensations and volitions and ideas? It seems clear that there are two ways of approaching the subject and that either may be taken separately. But this is not the place to develop metaphysical arguments. What is needed at the present moment is to explain the other type of machinery which Plato and Aristotle used and show how effectively it served the purpose.

One of the fundamental and persistent problems of psychology is presented by the fact that sensations occur. This class of events is approached by the modern psychologist as a complex situation and the mode of explanation is called " analysis of the stimulus-response situation." The reasons for this procedure seem to be two: first, that common sense suggests it as the most obvious; second, that it is traditional in some form or other throughout the history of psychological doctrines. But while the general description of sense-events can be given easily in this way, the real struggle begins when the details of the process are to be explained. In the following summary of the Greek standpoint the extreme refinements will be omitted and attention drawn only to the important points.

The complete process which results in a sense-event was regarded by all Greek writers as requiring three factors, namely beginning, middle, and end. It is necessary to state the facts in this bald manner because it was part of the Greek genius to deal with complicated matters in a way that is almost shocking in its simplicity. At the bottom of their deepest theories we find some simple unitary fact such as Being or Flowing, facts that have long since been overlaid by the later barbaric love of splendour which prefers to speak of the transcendental doctrine of ultimate reality, or the theory of a point-event continuum! Doubtless life is becoming more complicated every day, but it is none the less refreshing to look back at the times when the question at least was still intelligible. The Greeks were certainly adopting an a priori dogmatic method in declaring that everything must have a beginning, a middle, and an end; but we must not condemn this arrogance too harshly, for the method was frankly hypothetical, a mere trick of analysis, and it proved very useful. The immediate consequence was the doctrine of the *pneuma* ($\pi\nu\epsilon\tilde{\upsilon}\mu\alpha$), an extraordinarily subtle doctrine which pervaded the whole method and spirit of the psychological theories of all countries from the dawn of history to modern times.

The reader must understand that it is possible to have a doctrine which is very helpful and very long-lived but which is, strictly speaking, about nothing. This fact is an open secret in all learned societies, but it is not supposed to be known to the general public, unless the *Philosophy of the " As If "* is to be regarded as an official publication of this esoteric doctrine. Accordingly any curiosity about the real nature of this pneuma must be regarded as a mark of bad breeding; the really cultured man will understand that it is important to know the pneuma-doctrine but not to know any particular pneuma; in the best intellectual society etiquette required the Greek to talk as if there was a pneuma. Possibly, in the beginning, there was no great mystery about it. Pneuma was simply air, particularly air in motion. But the common people are very loose in their talk and provide a lot of work for philologists who insist on proper distinctions between things and names. Common people still use the word " wind " for the winds of heaven and for the phenomena of flatulence; the word flatulence reminds us that " flatus " can be used for inspiration (*afflatus*); for breath simply; for breath in speaking, when empty words are called *flatus vocis* by the mediaeval scholar and derided as " hot air " by the modern pupil. Similarly pneuma itself is an equivalent for air, wind, breath, the subtle airs of the Indian psychosophists, the vital spirits or airs, the soul as " anima," the Holy Spirit, and the divine element in the Hebrew doctrine of the created soul. Clearly this word is a portent of no small significance in the history of thought. It will be met at various points in the history of psychological doctrines and to avoid repetition the principal uses of the word as a technical term will be given at once in a brief summary.

Greek psychology was always a part of the philosophy of nature, and consequently in a broad sense it was a physiological doctrine concerned with some of the functions of organisms. The distinctive features of an organism are life and motion, sometimes to be regarded as one and sometimes distinguished according as the term "motion" becomes identical with change (metabolism) or is defined as local motion. Life is dependent on heat and this vital heat is contained in the first principle of life and growth, the vital substance itself, called connate pneuma (πνεῦμα σύμφυτον). As a principle of physical life and growth this pneuma or vital heat assists a variety of functions. It assists in digestion by converting the crude material into blood and pneuma, thus increasing itself and producing more pneuma which is found with the blood in all the veins and arteries. It is also increased by assimilating air taken in by breathing, and it tends to be progressively refined as it ascends from the digestive organs to the heart, or from the heart to the head. To cut a long story short we may say that as a physiological theory this doctrine of the pneuma travelled from Empedocles to Galen in unbroken development and appears in Galen (A.D. 200) in the final form which it retained until near the end of the eighteenth century. According to Galen there are three degrees of refinement of the pneuma: these are (a) the " natural " spirits active in the purely vegetative functions; (b) the " animal " spirits, located in the heart and regulating the beat of the heart and the bodily temperature; and (c) a special psychic pneuma in the brain and nerves to which are assigned sense, intellect, and will. In Galen's scheme both nerves and pneuma are employed, whereas originally the pneuma was the substitute for nerves. Before explaining this point it is necessary to go back to the earlier forms of this physiological hypothesis.

The works of Aristotle may be taken to represent the most mature theory of mental function prior to the discovery of the nerves. Proceeding in a methodical way to analyze the production of sensation according to the traditional five kinds, Aristotle describes the process as beginning from a stimulus which initiates movement of the pneuma in the organ of sense, continuing in the form of a motion of the pneuma mixed with the blood in the blood-vessels, and ending in the actual sensation at the heart. The fact that Aristotle made the heart the centre of mental functions is enough to make the modern reader turn away in disgust. To defend the doctrine would be absurd, but something ought to be said in defence of Aristotle. For those who asserted that the brain, or more accurately the contents of the skull, was the seat of the soul, either had at the time no adequate reason for the statement or relied on the belief that what is most important always necessarily occupies the top place. Plato, following Alkmaeon and the Pythagoreans, gave the divine part of man (Reason) a place nearest the heavens; the result was verbally correct but it may be doubted whether it had any genuine scientific basis, for Plato certainly regarded sensation as a function of the organism but lacked sufficient knowledge of the nervous system to make his theory include cerebral centres or processes. As against Plato and the ethical psychologists in general Aristotle could argue that logically a system which depended on the blood-vessels (nerves being unrecognized) must have its centre in the

[27]

heart; also that sensation must exist from the beginning of life and his own observations showed that the heart is " first to live and last to die." The root of the difference is probably to be found in the divergence of rival medical schools, for Empedocles also opposed the doctrines of Alkmaeon. Empedocles belonged to the Sicilian school and laid emphasis chiefly on breathing and circulation of the blood. Logically this could only lead to the conclusion that air and blood were the bearers of all functions and so to the actual decision that the bloodstream is the physiological agent in thinking.[3]

But as this is no more than special pleading the argument need not be continued, and perhaps Aristotle will not be harshly judged by a generation that no longer cares about the " seat of the soul " but finds its interest transferred to the glands that regulate personality! The most astonishing aspect of the pneuma-doctrine is the way in which it survived the discovery of the nerves. While the new anatomy compelled Galen to assign the psychic pneuma to the brain, the independent progress of philosophy compelled him to recognize that he was inventing a material agent to perform functions that had no exact quantity. A point often missed by students of Greek thought is indicated by the fact that the so-called " materialists," the Epicureans for example, assign a special kind of matter to the special functions called psychic. In other words the dispute was never between " materialism " and its opposite but between a method directed toward the organism as a whole and a method which recognized and supported the idea of the soul as a separate and separable thing. A scientific thinker who knows his own method and its proper limitations will not attempt to go beyond the data of organic life. In this respect Aristotle remained the " master of those who know," even when he became the servant of theologians. So too Epicurus, who in this respect keeps close to the Aristotelian tradition, was the moving spirit of the Italian Renaissance when it undertook to return to the fulness of life and the science of the complete organism. Galen was in a position not unlike that of Gall, the reputed founder of phrenology. For the days of Galen coincided with the development of a militant spiritualism. The new Platonists of the second century after Christ were not content with Platonic dualism; they would rather force the issue by attempting a cosmic spiritualism, which as usual

[29]

amounted to a more complete kind of dualism. Their service was to make clear how much and how little the understanding of experience owes to anatomy and physiology, how difficult it is to localize what cannot be defined in terms of extension, and in general to dispute the whole value of a quantitative division of the soul. Galen's eclectic mind was open to philosophical arguments and it is a credit to his genius that he saw the need for compromise. As Gall honestly tried to establish some unity between what he discovered about the brain and what was known about the mind, so Galen tried to make a classification of bodily functions which would include what we should now call the psychological types of behaviour. The net result was simply the assertion that there is in the organism something which acts like a mind and is in fact wholly unique.

Whether we employ the concept of the pneuma or a *vis nervosa* or any other bearer of the activity, we must sooner or later abandon the hypothesis and investigate the mind itself. Here we can only deal with the acts themselves and the beginning will be made by classifying these acts in some serviceable way. Science is born of practice, and even when there is no such antecedent practice as there was in the case of medicine or astronomy, there is always some floating body of opinion from which a start is made. We may assume that the general idea of sequence and order in mental operations grew up before reflective thought produced a reasoned system. The idea of five senses is traditional; so also are the ideas of sensation, imagination, memory, and reasoning; all that science can do is to revise and refine these notions. And, since so much contempt is poured at times on " faculty psychology," it may be worth while to note that Plato and Aristotle are both inclined to warn their readers against the notion of faculties. The Greek language more often indicates an act than a faculty; thought is the act of having in mind, memory is a safe-keeping, attention is holding the mind in a relation to something, reasoning (when not intuitive) is a process of calculation.

To arrange and classify the acts of the soul was the work of Aristotle. He was greatly assisted by the sporadic attempts of Plato who had contributed many points of permanent value to the traditional views. Among these special mention should be made of the following: the unity of mind was defended against earlier writers and it was contended that reason and not the end-organs is the real agent in sensation, for the senses are not separate agents in us like warriors in a Trojan horse; [4] memory is based on a principle of association which may be due to contiguity or similarity; suggestion or imitation is an important factor in the formation of character. Plato was anxious at all times to prove against the physical materialism of his day that the soul was an independent reality, but he recognized the importance of the body as an instrument and paid due attention to the fact that the soul acts with and through the body. But while it is possible to find in Plato many instances of keen psychological analysis, Aristotle was the first to arrange the data in the form of a special treatise and the formulae of Aristotle were the true starting point of scientific psychology.

The progress of anatomy and physiology has been so great in modern times that it has tended to distract attention from writers who were too early in time to employ these results. With the still more modern tendency to lay emphasis on biological points of view there has been created a new interest in work that depends mainly on the observation of functions and the description of behaviour. In this direction we find some writers, especially the few who still combine a knowledge of science with an ability to read Greek, looking back to the Greeks and chiefly to Aristotle with renewed admiration for the value of their contributions. In matters of history, politics, and ethics the great achievements of the Greeks have never been neglected or despised. In the natural sciences as a whole so much was lacking or positively erroneous that the new science created in the sixteenth century completely broke the tradition and after Galileo or Newton the only possible interest in Aristotelian physics was that of the pedant or the antiquarian. The name of Archimedes or that of Aristarchus was still worthy to be quoted, but even they could only deserve mention as pioneers in a work that was not actually completed. The case of psychology is curious. In so far as the Greeks were naturalists they anticipated the main trend of thought in modern times. In what concerns human nature the Renaissance achieved a return to the days of Thucydides, Plato, and Aristotle, rather than a new beginning. In the most recent times the experimental psychology of the laboratory has developed a method and an outlook which owes

[33]

nothing to the Greeks, but at the same time it does not cover the whole field and where ordinary observation or direct knowledge of human behaviour is the most important factor we may find ourselves still close to the Greek thinkers.

The general plan adopted by Plato and Aristotle is to regard the scale of nature as ascending from plants through plant-animals (zoophytes) and animals to man. The corresponding scale of functions is from the vegetative through the sensitive to the calculative or rational. This scheme really makes the affective or emotional elements most fundamental. Owing to the presence of ethical interests the acceptance of this fact was obscured, for it led directly to the conclusion that desires and feelings are at best to be controlled and, in the later trend toward asceticism, they are treated only as evils to be repressed or eliminated. This attitude, emphasized by some of the later Stoic and patristic writers, became so large a part of the western tradition that it obscured the way in which Plato utilized the emotions for the full development of human character, and practically annihilated Aristotle's doctrine in which the naturalistic study of the emotional life was never subordinated to ethical interests. Until very recent times text books of psychology all with one consent began with sensations and cognition; lately there has been a tendency to begin with the emotional life. Though we shall here follow the traditional method and discuss, first, the analysis of cognition, the reason for so doing is to dispose of the less important material first. For if we were to follow either the general plan of development which underlies the Greek study of mental life or take, first, the most fundamental parts, we should have to begin with the principles of action and the emotions.

2. THE ANALYSIS OF COGNITION

THOUGH we begin accordingly with sensations as the elementary facts, we are met at once with influences from the field of biological interests. The Greek writers considered that the primary interests in life, considered as fact and not in terms of ethical values, are eating, drinking, and reproduction. Food-seeking and mating are therefore the final causes of the development of the cognitive powers at the level of sensation. For these purposes the real value of sensation lies in the power which it confers

of making distinctions. Aristotle's formal definition of sensation is in these very terms: sensation is a capacity for discrimination.[5] Like a
flash of light the definition illuminates the
whole field of sense-activity. We see the animal using its senses to find the right food and
avoid the poisonous; we see the meaning of the
phrase that " touch is the fundamental sense "
as we watch the lowest kind of creature shrink
from the touch of a hand or adjust itself to heat
and cold; we see, too, how taste and smell con-
form to this definition and why sight and hearing are the most valuable senses because they
control the widest range of space, and this increasing range is itself the mark of the more
highly developed creatures.

The idea that knowledge is essentially book
learning seems to be a very modern view, probably derived from the mediaeval distinctions
between clerk and layman, with additional emphasis provided by the literary character of the
rather fantastic humanism of the sixteenth
century. The original and natural idea of
knowledge is that of " cunning " or the posses-
sion of wits. Odysseus is the original type of
thinker, a man of many ideas who could overcome the Cyclops and achieve a significant

[36]

triumph of mind over matter. Knowledge is thus a capacity for overcoming the difficulties of life and achieving success in this world. Through the influence of religion and of the priests it became also a requisite for success in the next world, and perhaps the knowledge of secret symbols and mystic phrases is the real root of all book learning, the genesis and justification of "scriptures." So we need not be surprised to learn that such naive people as the Greeks unconsciously proclaimed the fundamental principles of biological pragmatism. To prove this point it is only necessary to consider carefully the following passage in Aristotle's *Ethics*.

In the tenth chapter of the third book of the *Nicomachean Ethics* Aristotle discusses the moral virtue of restraint, σωφροσύνη, (*sophrosyne*), this and courage being the two virtues which show most clearly how and when the natural impulses require control. Obviously we may say that this control is most needed when pleasure is too tempting or when suffering makes men shirk their painful duties. But while we generally say that restraint must be used in the exercise of the senses, there seem to be some cases which are not regular, especially hearing. For ordinary people never use the term " vicious " in reference to people who are too fond of music and theatres; this seems to be a case where no vice is possible, and yet there are possible exceptions. Hearing is very much like smell in this respect; both acquire a moral significance " by accident " as Aristotle would say, or as we say because they are " conditioned." The pleasure which some persons derive from sounds or smells is really a self-indulgence " because by these means they acquire recollection of the objects of desire " (*E.N.*, 1118a6). The moral quality therefore arises from a psychological complication. Aristotle proceeds to make the point clear by considering animals, where there is no danger of confusing the natural stimulus and the supposed " aesthetic " value. Animals other than men, he says, like the smell of food when they are hungry; but the hounds only care for the smell of an animal because it is connected with eating and, as it were, generates the sense of eating; the lion does not attend to the lowing of the oxen to study the musical pitch nor even its " meaning " in the sense that speech may be interpreted; for the lion the sound " means " nothing but proximity and moreover it is not so much proximity of the ox as proximity of a meal.[6]

This is a most illuminating passage. It shows an astonishing breadth of vision. Through it we catch a glimpse of the whole evolution of the mind from the most primitive responses up to the most highly evolved forms of meaning. It offers almost irresistible temptations to expand and comment on its suggestiveness as the hint of possible theories of the growth of the mind and conditioned reflexes and sublimation and many other modern topics. These flashes of insight and terse epitomes of doctrine have made Aristotle the most apt material for the commentators of all ages, but commentary is not our present business and we must leave the readers to value the quotation for themselves.

Enough has been said to show how Aristotle regards sensation as primarily a form of organic response which enables a creature to make the distinctions necessary for its various adaptations. All activity begins at the level of merely living (τὸ ζῆν); but the Greek regards this as the first step toward a higher form, the life that is lived well and is made the object of conscious striving after the good things of this world, principally health and sanity. The doctrine of development which is the basis of the psychological scheme now becomes a complex form of the doctrine of motion. The agent in sensation is the pneuma described above, but the mode of action is movement ($\kappa\acute{\iota}\nu\eta\sigma\iota\varsigma$) and when the functions themselves are analyzed or described the modes of motion become most important. A sensation regarded as a positive event is a mode of motion which takes place in the pneuma and ends by producing the "appearance" of an object in the mind. This is a very vague statement, but it is doubtful whether anything more definite can be said about the origin of sensations. While the earlier Greeks attempted to be more precise and laid down such principles as "by like we know like," or asserted an influx of atoms to be the real explanation of sensation, Plato and Aristotle saw the futility of all these efforts. The fact that all sensation seems to require an external stimulus led to the intermediate type of theory which is content to say that sensation is a form of impression. As the seal does not leave any part of itself in the wax but does leave its impression ($\tau\acute{\upsilon}\pi\omega\sigma\iota\varsigma$), so the object might be said to "impress" the mind. But what are these factors really? Is the mind really anything like wax, and can it have such " dents and grooves " as the word " impression " really ought to indicate? Plato certainly felt that the phrase was only a metaphor, a rather loose way of illustrating the idea that in sensation the mind is relatively passive. In Aristotle we find discontent more openly expressed. When we perceive a stone, the stone at any rate is not in the soul. How can we express this fact of impression? The formula which is at last reached runs thus: the sense is receptive of the form without the matter.[7] This means that the meeting of outer and inner factors is not a deposit of some material thing in a substance called soul, but is a generation of a new activity and the beginning of a new series of events. So in the end Aristotle would regard sensation as a qualitative change, a mode of motion which is an activity, and simply an " awareness." In this he was followed by the Stoics and we may reckon this outcome as a decisive formulation of the important doctrine that sensation must be regarded as elementary psychic activity.

Plato gave very little time or attention to the separate senses and their physiological conditions. Aristotle on the contrary devotes a great part of his treatise on the soul to minute details of the structure and function of each sense. But, as was stated above, beyond the interest thus shown in a proper scientific approach and the influence exerted by this pattern on all later psychological works, there is nothing of sufficient value to justify the reproduction of this part of the work. The theory progressed to a large extent independent of the details and has survived the changes brought by later investigations. This theory depends on a few simple deductions, and first comes the deduction from unity of consciousness. While we can speak of the senses separately we cannot admit that this is more than a convenient abstraction. As Plato reminded his generation (quoting an earlier writer) it is the *mind* that sees, the *mind* that hears. Aristotle makes this doctrine of centralization more exact by proceeding from the special senses to the "common sense." As each sense has its peculiar place or "sensorium," so we must suppose that the centre is a place. Aristotle named it the common sensorium ($\kappa o \iota \nu \grave{o} \nu \ a \grave{\iota} \sigma \theta \eta \tau \acute{\eta} \rho \iota o \nu$). The modern phrase " common sense " is not used with much reference to this origin, but it is in fact a rather accurate representation of the original idea. For the common sensorium is a sort of mind,

[42]

not as intellect but as a general meeting place of sense-experiences. Aristotle located it in the heart (cp. p. 27), but the place is of little importance from the point of view of the function. When we speak only in terms of action, the mind is to be regarded as the " place of forms " and these forms are all the phenomena of experience which we shall find summed up at last as the " passive intellect."

The term " motion " in the Greek writers denotes not only translation from place to place but also transition from one condition to another. It can be used accordingly either for the actual transmission of a stimulus from the outside to the inside, as from the eye to the brain (Plato) or heart (Aristotle), or for transition from pleasure to pain. Both interpretations seem to be employed in the psychological scale, for at first the motion is positive and physiological but later it becomes metaphorical. The scale of functions is developed accordingly. The first positive motion excited by a presented object is a sensation or at least the external aspect of a sensation; where the object is not still active, there may be a " decaying sensation," [8] a kind of after-effect persisting in the organ; this is imagination (φαντασία); since

[43]

this is a residuum from the moment of perception and outlasts the exact time of impression, it may be described as "abiding," and this is the root idea of the word memory ($\mu\nu\dot\eta\mu\eta$). The whole idea and the analogy which it suggests between positive sensations and the subsequent retention is so neatly expressed by Shelley that the lines may fitly be quoted:

> Music, when soft voices die,
> Vibrates in the memory;
> And so thy thoughts, when thou art gone,
> Love itself shall slumber on.

A brief statement made for practical purposes in the *Posterior Analytics* sums up Aristotle's view of the genesis of experience.[9] What is called experience is the product of many memory-traces; all that is necessary is that some fleeting impression should be stopped in its flight and, as when one soldier halts in the flight of an army, the rest will gather round. In this Aristotle was following Plato's leadership. The flux of sensations had been emphasized by Heraclitus and exploited by the Sophists. But it is absurd to say there is no such thing as knowledge, more especially when we regard this statement as something which everyone knows!

The serious thinker undertakes to explain knowledge and not explain it away; his task is not either metaphysics or epistemology but plain scientific analysis. Taking this position both Plato and Aristotle see that the crucial point is memory and memory is a given fact about which there can be no honest dispute. This fact has to be accepted although the explanation of its mechanism may be difficult or impossible. Modern psychologists may study in more detail the types of memory or the function of meaning in memory or ways of improving the memory, but they one and all accept the elementary facts of memory and reduce it to the terms of our Greek psychologists, namely persistence of the traces of earlier experiences.

In the *Phaedo* Plato made the first statement of what is called the law of association. Here he uses the relations of contiguity and similarity; the sight of the lyre suggests the idea of its player, or the sight of Simmias suggests his companion Cebes; also a picture of an object or a person recalls the original. But Plato makes no further attempt to work out the detail of the process. He implies in the *Republic* that the process of experience produces unconscious memories (v.p.80), but memory itself he

[45]

treats as irrefutable proof of the soul's activity and accordingly emphasizes the power of the mind to *think* about one thing when the senses are affected by another. Memory thus becomes a mystery demanding faith in the transcendence of all sensuous existence and ultimately the belief that all knowing is pure activity. This view, stubbornly refusing to admit that knowledge can be analyzed into impressions and explained as the mere deposit of sense experiences, became a tremendous influence in the later history of thought. It was however a clear case of subordinating explanation to a foreign purpose. Plato's interest in memory was directed by his conception of Anamnesis as the only possible explanation of the origin of concepts and at the same time a proof that

The soul that rises with us, our life's star,
Hath had elsewhere its setting and
cometh from afar.

On this point the contrast between Plato and Aristotle is very marked. Aristotle confines himself to empirical analysis and makes a careful statement of the genesis and nature of memory. That he realized the importance of the subject is shown by the fact that he wrote a special treatise on memory and recollection.[10] The root of the whole matter is to be found in the doctrine of imagination, and this must first be explained. Aristotle inherited the problem of all the Platonists, namely the necessity of explaining coherently the facts of reception, retention, and revival of experiences. The reception is explained by the doctrine of the senses, which is little more than a description of the visible organs with the necessary assumption that "somehow" in them the physical becomes psychic, the movement becomes sensation. Retention is a more difficult problem because the process is less objective and the theory must limit itself to a judicious combination of the supposed facts. Plato had already indicated that the essential factor in memory is the appearance of the mental object when the physical object is not present and cannot be an active stimulus. This certainly happens, but further analysis shows that this description will apply to a whole class of events. If we consider the whole class we can arrange the different groups in a progressive order; after the sensation comes the residual motion constituting the image, then the latent disposition which causes one image to revive another by association, then the kinds of imagery which generate themselves in abnormal states and become illusions, and finally the purposive revival which is achieved by using the same machinery and is called recollection.

The student of Aristotle always has to remember that every process of explanation is reducible to the elements called matter and form. Wherever change occurs there is a transition from an earlier to a later state of being; the marble becomes the statue, the acorn becomes the oak, the emotions become the character. While these processes are the same in outward appearance, they differ in one important respect. The statue is produced by the sculptor working from without; art is external and superficial, for it changes only the surface. But the oak is produced by nature, a greater artist working from within, no longer superficial but penetrating the inmost being of its material. Character, Aristotle regarded as an example of the most deep and penetrating change, for the agent by his own acts changes himself; to build a house is to make something external and detachable, but to build a character is to re-make the builder himself.

Returning to the problem of memory with this

general scheme in mind, we see that Aristotle's problem is to provide the kind of material which can be used at each stage of the process from sensation to purposive recollection. He thinks this can be done by translating sensation into motion and assuming that the inner motion can be aroused from either end, that is, either by the external object or the inner principle of activity. The advantages of this scheme are proved, according to Aristotle, by the fact that with its aid a number of experiences can be correlated and explained.

We may consider first the nature of memory. Animals appear to remember, but probably they do not reason; if memory is in their case the periodic revival of perceptions in the form of imagery, we have all the explanation needed. Man is a superior animal and, accordingly, acts sometimes like the other animals and sometimes in a distinct manner. When he is drunk or asleep or disturbed by passion the human animal acts without reason and the mental processes become more like those of other animals. The general character of this lower type of action is that it tends to be mechanical, and memory is then no more than the habit of the organism which has been produced by the order of experiences. This is what is meant by the term " association of ideas," but it is important to notice that Aristotle states his doctrine not as an association of " ideas " but as a connection of " motions." [11] The criticisms which James and Bradley have directed against the theory of association would not apply to Aristotle's doctrine. Aristotle says " mental movements in these instances are identical in some cases, in others simultaneous with the desired experience, and in other cases they involve a portion of it, so that there is a small remainder whose stimulation ensues." In other words the memory of an object X occurs when there is a revival of the motion x in which it was originally given, or when a motion y occurs and develops into x, or when a part of x is first aroused and becomes the complete whole x.

If this is the actual process which constitutes memory, it is easy to explain recollection; for it will be the reflective use of this machinery. When the motion re-establishes itself there is no need for further effort; the cases to be considered are those in which there is a conscious effort to recall. The possibility of recollection does not depend on any mysterious power of the soul but on the simple fact that we remember some things better than others; those which are more easily remembered can be used to revive the others. " When we recollect we awaken certain antecedent processes and continue this until we call up that particular experience, after which the desired one is wont to appear. That is the reason why we hunt through a series in thought, beginning with an object presented before us, or with something else, or with an object that is similar, or opposite or contiguous." In this passage Aristotle gives the original statement of the " laws of association " and also the rules of that *memoria technica* or art of recollection which the ancients practiced with all the fervour that marks the modern pursuit of Pelmanism.

The reader will have noticed in this account of memory that the distinction between spontaneous recurrence and purposive recall of images is due to the different proportions in which passivity and activity are mixed. Aristotle regards the events called experience as the " matter " of thought; he does not suppose that these events can themselves produce the mind. In more modern language Aristotle would insist that experience gives the content of thought, but the act of thought is underived. There are accordingly two ways of regarding all acts of mind, except the two limiting terms sense and reason. Both sense and reason in Aristotle are intuitive; when we see a colour we have an immediate datum which is not analyzable, for the physical basis of colour is not an explanation of the colour-sense; similarly when we see a truth we have the same kind of immediacy and Aristotle expresses this by saying that reason, as it were, touches its object.

Within the limits of psychology, then, the two extremes, sense and reason, have no proper explanations. Between the extremes every stage involves a proportionate mixture of act and content, and explanation consists very largely in analyzing each stage into these factors. If we consider the processes themselves we shall find that they differ according as the preponderance belongs to the incoming or the outgoing activity, just as modern psychologists have distinguished between what is peripherally excited and what is centrally excited. The imagination is the central pivot on which Aristotle makes his scientific psychology turn. The common or central sense receives and integrates the data of the special senses. The sensations as pure events can only be what they are, and as such they are always real and neither true nor false. The imagination is one step removed from this primitive reality; it may occur under conditions that are determined by inner states, either physiological or mental. It is important, therefore, to consider the origin and nature of illusions, hallucinations, and all other diseases of the imagination ($\phi\alpha\nu\tau\alpha\sigma\iota\alpha$). Nearest to the act of sensation and significant as proof of its persistence are the after-images which Aristotle had carefully observed. "Actual sensation is a kind of qualitative change. Consequently this condition is found in the sense-organs not only during the process of sensation, but also after the process has ceased, and in their inner depths as well as on the surface. This becomes evident when we have a sensation that continues over some time. For when we turn our senses to something else, the original sensation persists, as e.g., when we turn from the sun to a dark object. The result is that one sees nothing owing to the fact that the sense-process stimulated by the light, still lurks in the eyes. And if one looks a long time at a single colour,

whether it be white or green, things appear to
be similarly coloured wherever we turn our
eyes. Again if we look at the sun or some
bright object and then shut our eyes, there appears to sharp observation, in the direct line
which vision employs, first of all a colour like
the actual one, which then changes to scarlet,
then to purple, until it passes into blackness and
vanishes." [12] These phenomena, here so faithfully observed and described, have become the
property of all subsequent psychology under
the title of " positive or negative after images."
In Aristotle's eyes their chief value was that
they proved the persistence of the inner states;
incidentally they serve to explain the images in
dreams and other states analogous to dreams.

Images are the last product of sensation and
the first material of thought. Since they can be
revived without external agency they are capable of being united in new forms, and this is the
creative imagination of the artist. A short step
from this brings us to thought, the use of concepts and the whole range of the reasoning faculty. Imagination is impossible without sensation and conceptual thought is impossible without imagination.[13] Thus we reach the highest
limit of the cognitive powers, and so far as con-

cerns the psychology of reasoning Aristotle has said his last word. In declaring thought impossible without imagination Aristotle subscribes to a theory which is truly empirical, but not limited to sensationalism. Since the reason is really the "place of forms" and the act of reasoning is selection and rejection of images, the reason must itself be an immanent power. But then we come back to the old puzzle of origins. We ask Whence came the soul? or Whence came life? Apparently Aristotle's answer was essentially that which Leibnitz restated in the phrase "the intellect is innate to itself." In modern terms we should say that in the course of development it supervenes or emerges, which is useful because it is a reminder, at the end of the book on "the soul," that after all the soul had been the subject of the discussion all the time. Many psychologists seem to forget that a science deals with the parts of a whole and therefore always assumes but never needs to discuss the whole itself. There is no science of the Universe, but all sciences presuppose the Universe. If psychology is not a science of the soul but only of phenomena, that is true mainly because it presupposes the soul as the basis of the phenomena.

II. PSYCHOLOGY OF CONDUCT

SO far we have been concerned with what is known generally as the psychology of cognition. As begun by Plato and developed by Aristotle this part of the work has been extraordinarily stable; at any rate it has been faithfully copied for the best part of twenty two hundred years. As space will not permit any more expansion of this topic further details will be omitted. The complementary part of Greek psychology is concerned with volition, and became known to later writers as "the theory of the active powers." This term is unfortunate, for it implies that in cognition the mind is merely passive and receptive, which was not the standpoint either of Plato or Aristotle. It will be more appropriate to use the phrase "psychology of conduct" for this part of the theory, since it is concerned with those powers which belong distinctively to the outward actions or behaviour of sentient organisms.

Following the lead of Socrates Plato undertook to formulate a theory of the good life.

Both Plato and Aristotle assume as an axiom that the good life is that which manifests the highest powers of man and in this sense it will be a life regulated by reason. But Plato taught and Aristotle explicitly affirms that the understanding does not move to action. The organic force in life is neither identical with nor separate from the reason; it is a component part of the whole psychic mechanism and its differentiation runs parallel with the ascending scale of psychic development. Since the concrete individual is a rational animal, there is a sense in which the elements of character are to be found in the nature of animals, though there is no exact sense in which the term conduct or character would be applied to animals by Plato or Aristotle.

Plato's interest is so much confined to human beings and their welfare that he says very little about the lower types of life except in illustration of this theme. The main object of Plato's psychology of conduct is to show how life may become well ordered and be controlled by the conscious apprehension of principles. He illustrates this mainly by tracing the development from childhood to maturity, assuming an ideal type of maturity as the regulative idea of his description. The whole plan of this development is stated as a process of education and will be treated later in discussing the forms of applied psychology (pp. 75–105). But it is necessary to note here that Plato bases the whole development on an organic principle which he calls, somewhat poetically, *Eros*. This principle, afterwards made notorious as " Platonic love," is the fundamental driving force in nature. In its most primitive form it is sexual desire, which leads every creature to seek its mate and reproduce its kind. In a wider sense it is the general desire for all forms of satisfaction, physical or mental. In its highest manifestation it is described as that divine discontent which can only be satisfied by the vision of Truth and Beauty (see pp. 96–99).

Beyond recognizing this general principle of activity Plato does little to explain the nature of the original forces in life. He accepts the view of development which puts first the functions of nutrition, then sensation, and finally reason. As he is more concerned to show the relation between impulse and restraint than to write a scientific treatise, he works out a parallel between the structure of the body and the types of activity. Desire (ἐπιθυμία) is associated with the primary activities, hunger, thirst, and sex; it is accordingly represented by the " belly and the members," and is a very powerful incentive to action. St. Paul and the Christian fathers made this doctrine famous by recognizing a law in the members which wars against the higher law of reason. In Plato this element of desire tends to express itself through all the senses, so that it includes the desire of the eyes and the pride of life. In the fourth book of the *Republic* Leontius is led astray by the desire to look upon the corpses of the criminals, and this desire is so strong that it overcomes the sense of propriety which it outrages.[14] Plato does not teach that desire and principles are always opposed, but he maintains that they may at any time come into conflict; they are distinct sources of action and it is only in the noblest characters that desire works in harmony with reason. This so-called dualism in Plato is in fact a very penetrating analysis of what is called the moral conflict. The peculiarities of Plato's method and language should not blind us to the fact that he is a keen student of human nature and a shrewd observer of experience, in all its variety.

[59]

Next to desire Plato puts a factor named θυμός, usually called " the spirited element." The term has no exact equivalent in our language, but it has an exact meaning and its importance is generally overlooked. In the development of character there is a stage which is reached before reflective reason is developed. We may see it in the schoolboy who has strong but not very well-defined sentiments of loyalty, with a readiness to fight anyone who does not agree with him. We see it in the politician who stands by the principle " my country right or wrong." Plato seems to have a liking for this quality, which he associates with pugnacity by making it the essential mark of those who have to fight for the maintenance of law and order. Perhaps after the age of the Sophists there was a reaction in Plato's mind against all quibblers and a sturdy respect for the men of action about whom it might be said " theirs not to reason why, theirs but to do and die." But, whatever the explanation may be, Plato here again has skilfully depicted a type and at the same time defined an element in human nature, the stubborn unquestioning tenacity of principles which is the pride of the man of action and the despair of all sceptics and theorists.

The desires and the senses are coextensive with life; they are the minimum required to explain the actions of animals and men. It may be that some human beings really develop no other principles of action, and, as the Christian hymn expresses it, "like brutes they live, like brutes they die." In any case the animal and the child neither have nor need any other equipment. The "spirited element" comes at a higher level because it implies opinions about what is right and wrong, though we must not forget that the word "opinion" is for the Greek a somewhat contemptuous term for obscure ideas that are incomplete and fall short of reasoned accuracy. The highest level of life is that degree of mental development at which the ideas are clear and distinct, the level of reason in the proper sense, the well grounded knowledge of good and evil. Plato's rationalism has been unfortunately distorted into "intellectualism," probably because we are hardly able any longer to rid ourselves of the notion that reason means intellect and intellect means academic superiority. If we go back to the days of Plato, when an "academy" was a novelty and books were almost non-existent, if we could think again of education as the life-long struggle of the individual to see life steadily and see it whole, this error might cease to be perpetuated. Yet even in Plato's time some one seems to have erred. For when Socrates said Virtue is Knowledge he must have meant that right action depends on right convictions; yet Aristotle finds it necessary to point out that desire could not be said to overthrow "scientific" knowledge and that Socrates was wrong if he meant that right action is the same thing as knowing the scientific facts. Most probably Socrates meant very much what Plato and all the great reformers have meant, namely, that those to whom the vision of the good has been revealed can thereafter see nothing else. The goal of the Platonic development of character has been rightly interpreted by all the mystics, including Spinoza, not as an accumulation of knowledge but as complete vision, "the master light of all our seeing."

When we turn to Aristotle we find the same ideas and the same conclusions, but the expansive poetry has disappeared and we hear the language of the great naturalist talking more like a behaviourist than a poet. As Aristotle's formulae are more akin to modern psychology, it will be necessary to supplement the Platonic version by summing up the main points in Aristotle's treatment of conduct.

Remembering his general scheme of development with its sequence of nutritive, sensitive, and rational "souls," Aristotle selects a term which will serve as a common denominator for all biological activity, just as the term irritability is used in modern physiology for the most elementary form of living response to stimulus. The term used by Aristotle is *orexis*, (ὄρεξις), which means reaching after or striving after, and is equivalent to the Latin *conatus,* from which we get the word that has come into general use in recent times, "conation." This orectic activity is as fundamental as life itself and persists through the whole range of animal and human development. In its own nature it remains constant, an ever present dynamic element, but as the organism develops additional powers it appears in more complex forms and is modified by the factors which co-operate with it. At the level of the primary impulses *orexis* is what the Latin writers correctly call *appetitus*. Appetite has survived to the present day as a special word for food-seeking; we also use it metaphorically to denote any irrational pursuit of satisfaction and in scientific language it retains the same significance, though usually written " appetition." The philosophers of the sixteenth century who wrote in Latin used " appetitus " for any relation which implied a " movement toward," as for example magnetic attractions, the attractions of the stone by the earth toward which it falls (*lapis petit terram*), or the attraction of an animal by the edible plant. This was a very justifiable use of the term and its history thus serves to show how it became a general word for the whole range of activities which lead to some state of rest or satisfaction.

When we proceed to correlate this original activity with each level of biological development we have to consider how it may vary according as the modifying factor is sensation, imagination, or reason. Conation and sensation constitute the lowest level, the Platonic " desire." The object is first apprehended by the senses; appetite accounts for the movement by which it is appropriated, as a hungry dog seizes a bone. But the dog may be hungry when there is no bone; its desire is vain and it wanders aimlessly, until it is led by habit to its customary feeding place. We may assume that some inner motion has taken place and restores an image of the food or the place where the food should be, for Aristotle thinks animals possess this kind of imagination. The evidence for this is not very exact in the case of animals, but in man the phenomenon in question is called wish. The condition called " wishing for something " is a complex state in which we have conation united with an image of the object which could, if present, give satisfaction to desire. Wishing is a kind of affirmative judgment, but it is very incomplete. As a judgment, or what the modern writer would call a " yes-attitude," wish is the possible source of deliberation. Sometimes we have purely imaginative wishes and do not entertain them seriously enough to work out all that is implied in attainment; sometimes, as Aristotle notes, wish is incompatible with any action; for we may wish that a person will win a prize but the conditions of fulfillment (short of bribery and corruption) are out of our power. When the wish is directed to an end which might be obtained by further action, the process of reflecting on the means is the natural evolution of the impulse. Here reason as power of calculation comes into action and we are said to deliberate. The conclusion of this process may be positive or negative, acceptance

[65]

or rejection, but in either case it is choice; and Aristotle defines choice as conation refined by deliberation, which is the same as rational pursuit of ends.[15] Here again it must be noted that " rational" does not mean wise or good, but merely deliberate. Life is ruled by reason in the sense that men calculate; if the desire is for wealth and the way of attainment is murder, the choice is " rational." Because he saw this point and had no faith in the doctrine that men seek only the good, Hobbes very correctly quotes the Aristotelian definition when he says that " will is the last appetite." Aristotle as a psychologist emphasizes the fact that desire is not for the good in itself; it may be for the apparent good; sometimes men desire the good, but more often "men call good that which they desire," a point which was restored to modern thought by Machiavelli. Plato and Aristotle were always in agreement on this point, that desire has for its object the desired; whether that which is desired is good or bad in a wider sense depends on whether the individual has been trained to make the right kind of choice. To this question of training or education Plato devoted much thought and his plan will be considered separately. Aristotle wrote no treatise on education but laid down certain principles defining the nature and limits of human development.

Some one in the days of Aristotle seems to have objected that education involves changing a person's nature, and nature is not capable of change. You may throw a stone upward a thousand times, but it always comes down; it never learns to go up; and by analogy all other things merely manifest their natures, are not really capable of change, and might as well be left to develop themselves.[16] This plausible argument is rejected by Aristotle on the ground that what is true in mechanics is not true in biology. Nature is not a thing but a process; growth is a series of minute increments and the total result is the product of these increments. Training is not a mechanical process like the projection of a stone but a form of conditioning, making growth more possible in one direction and less possible in another. Aristotle recognizes that the possibilities of change are very limited; but we must not argue that because education will not do everything therefore it can do nothing. Some human beings are devoid of all capacity to learn: they are maimed at the start and cannot run the race; others

[67]

have congenital defects that will prevent them from going very far; a few are divinely favoured and have so much natural goodness (εὐφυΐα) that they hardly need to be trained at all. Yet making allowance for all the varieties of human nature, there is always need for the acquisition of self-control and conscious principles of action. Nature endows the young with impulses and sensations; it does not give them a knowledge of social regulations or innate ideas of law, and education is essentially the making of good citizens.

We detect here a difference between Aristotle and Plato. Disregarding the Idea of the Good and the question of eternal and immutable Justice, Aristotle inclines to limit his theory to the sphere of social adjustment. He defines ethics expressly as the sphere of praise and blame, considering that a good man is one who does the things that are praised and a bad man is one who does the opposite. In other words good and bad, in the ethical sense, are forms of conduct which have been discovered in the course of human experience and the individual has to learn this wider law of life which belongs to the City; for the City (πόλις, *Polis*) embodies a greater experience than his own and traditions

[68]

or laws are a kind of purified reason, historically tested and matured, enthroned above the storms of passion. With this point of view it is easy for Aristotle to find a simple rational formula for all training. The keyword is habituation. All things that grow tend to form habits and these habits are the product of the influences brought to bear on them. Plants and animals need not be considered, as no one wishes to educate them; slaves, too, should be included in this class. Confining our attention to the prospective citizen we find that the three factors which must be kept in mind are nature, habit, and reason. Nature gives the endowment; habit controls the lines of growth; reason adopts the law when it is comprehended and so becomes an independent principle of conduct.[17] The last term might seem to be an illogical addition, but that is far from the case. Aristotle is not proposing to produce automata; habituation is only a middle term; the goal of training is to produce agents, creators, who have the " second nature," and are capable of living by a law that has become their own inner selves.

Aristotle and Plato agree that the typical form of human development is from the impulsive stage to the regulative or rational. "Children and animals live according to their feelings" is the brief dictum of Aristotle. But Aristotle is more attentive to the details which this theory implies and carefully distinguishes the types which occur according to the ratio between impulse and reason in the individual's character. Every virtue is an acquired state (ἕξις) and should therefore operate at any time without conflict. The temperate man who has control of his desires presents the appearance of overcoming temptations easily, not because he is not sensible of the temptation but because he has proper control of his passions. The brave man is the one who acts bravely in an emergency, not because he is ready to rush blindly into danger but because his sense of duty enables him to grasp the situation promptly and his natural fears are dominated by the habit of doing what is right in such crises. Such men are ruled by principles, but they are ideal types; the majority will at least hesitate sometimes and sometimes fail altogether. The passions are very deeply rooted and self-preservation is nature's first law. It is not surprising, then, that in the moment of trial there is often a startling relapse; the respectable citizen turns out to be in secret a drunkard, or the reputed hero is found to have deserted his comrade in battle. Aristotle has a keen sense for this great fact, that vices are really relapses into more primitive types of conduct. Temperance and courage are put first in the list of virtues because they demand the transformation of our animal natures into human and civil life. The life of the city, civilization, urbanity, politeness are all sources of perpetual strain upon the human being, still only partly able to control the tiger and the lion hidden under his skin.

Complete virtue, then, is complete control of the impulses by the deliberative or calculative reason. A person capable of this type of behaviour is said to be master of himself, to keep himself well in hand ($\dot{\epsilon}\gamma\kappa\rho\alpha\tau\dot{\eta}s$). In more psychological language we might say that such a person has a strong will. The divergences from this type are measured by the degree of conflict. In some cases we see the intention beginning to work in one direction and then suddenly the behaviour swerves to another direction. It is a case of mental paralysis; for in just the same way, says Aristotle, we see the paralytic begin a movement toward a particular end and then the afflicted limb swerves the opposite way. In the case of Leontius (v. p. 59) Plato gave a concrete example; Aristotle states the general formula. The unreliable character or the weak will is called ἀκρατής and his affliction is known as ἀκρασία. Sometimes this state is due to want of proper inhibition, which is a necessary step to deliberation; the result is then the impulsive type, quickly overcome by suggestion, meaning well but not often acting well. Sometimes the type is really the reverse; the deliberation is protracted, the rightness of the act is known, but the choice is not converted into action. These types correspond to the modern distinction of impulsive will and obstructed will. As the relation between impulse and calculation gradually becomes such that the individual gives up the attempt to maintain his principles, there emerges a third type, the incorrigible, and wholly corrupt, the unprincipled man (ἀκόλα-στος). Outwardly this is a strong and stable type. Like Milton's Satan he says "Evil be thou my good," and is for ever fallen. Morally this is the lowest type, but psychologically it exhibits strength because it is no longer divided against itself.[18]

According to Aristotle all moral choice involves conscious grasp of principles. This implies a universal rule, and therefore conduct depends on a procedure which is syllogistic. In the normal case of right action, the person knows the rule and brings the particular case under it, as for example "one ought to taste what is sweet" and "this is a sweet thing": from which, by virtue of the harmony between principle and desire, there follows the conclusion, which is in the practical syllogism not a verbal conclusion but the act itself. In the case of yielding to temptation the person may preserve an apparent rationality by using a rule which is itself suggested by the desire. If we assume that reason says in a particular case, "sweet things ought to be avoided" but this is opposed by a desire for sweet things, the individual invents for himself an argument such as "all sweet things are pleasant," and with this irrelevant principle justifies the action which his desires suggest. The wish is father to the thought. Here Aristotle very neatly formulated the process of self-sophistication or rationalization, for the universal premise used to make the argument is really prompted by the desire which moves to action. Animals, according to Aristotle, cannot be said to yield to temptation because they do not use general principles of conduct. Human beings, because they have reason, are able to compromise: they justify the satisfaction of desire by constructing a spurious argument which serves to excuse the action.

III. APPLIED PSYCHOLOGY

1. EDUCATION

THE fifth century before Christ closed with a movement variously denoted as the age of the Sophists or the Greek Enlightenment. Omitting its other features as irrelevant to our purpose, we must emphasize the significant fact that its keynote was humanism. In this case, as in many other similar periods of history, humanism was a form of retrenchment; it was primarily negative, refusing to accept anything which it regarded as transcendent and speculative. The corresponding positive movement was empirical in character, analogous to the nominalism of the twelfth century and the empiricism of the eighteenth century in European thought. Empiricism in all these cases led to more careful investigation of the human individual's power to apprehend and interpret his world. In other words, empiricism by its very nature tends to promote a psychological attitude of mind and

[75]

even when the outcome is not a distinct contribution to pure psychology there is a tendency to review all the activities of man and explain them in the terms of the current psychology.

The well known formula of Protagoras, "man is the measure of all things," is a brief epitome of this doctrine. Socrates and his successors, Plato and Aristotle, repudiate the doctrine as a final and complete philosophy of life; but it left its mark on Greek speculative thought. As we see from Plato's *Theaetetus*, it was necessary to analyze the whole range of mental activity before the function of the senses could be properly estimated. It was no less necessary to reconstruct the general theory of human activity, both individual and social, before a different philosophy of life could be regarded as well established. In this effort to reconstruct philosophy there is accordingly a strong vein of psychological analysis which runs through the whole doctrine of man and his activities. To this we may give the name of applied psychology, because the general psychological outlook is here used to justify and explain ethical and political teaching.

The word "ethics" is specially significant in this connection. As many writers have pointed out, it is peculiarly Greek. The Roman naturally spoke of morals, thinking first of the *mores* or established customs, and holding that the first law of conduct was the maintenance of the social and legal traditions. Greek individualism tended to less rigid conservatism; and, whatever may have been the resentment felt against innovations, the necessity of allowing character (ἦθος, *ēthos*) to develop spontaneously seems never to have been doubted. Every creature has its own particular character and the community has a character which sums up and exhibits collectively the types of individual life. So Plato can say that the State is the individual " writ large," and at the same time evolve a plan by which the community can so influence the individual that the approved type of character will be perpetuated.

When Plato considers the State from the point of view of practical legislation he assumes as his basis the broad biological concepts of nature and nurture. Every organism has a nature; it grows by some kind of assimilation, in fact it " grows by what it feeds on," and there is room for a science of growth in the case of human beings no less than with plants or animals. Eugenics came into existence among the

Greeks as a product of their naturalism; they instinctively looked for the conditions of well-being (εὐγένεια) and saw that the mind needed and used its nourishment with results as sure as those known to the breeder of plants or animals. Nature is not in man's control, so attention must be paid to nurture (τροφή). Guided by this principle Plato considers what are somewhat metaphorically called principles of education. We need not quarrel with the phrase so long as it does not make us forget that this " education " is a life-long process of development controlled from first to last by the tone of the whole community and the opportunities it supplies for better or worse results. Defined in this way education becomes both psychological and social; in attempting to present an orderly scheme of education Plato was inevitably drawn toward social psychology. We do not find in Plato's works a separate treatise on the psychology of education or the psychology of society, but we find life interpreted from a psychological point of view, partly as growth of the mind and partly as the relation between minds. The age of specialization had not yet come; what the Greeks said of the primitive earth was true of their own sci-

ences, that "all things were together." But if
we carefully sift out this wonderful collection
of seeds we find some of each kind, and many
of the psychological kind. A few samples will
show that what the Greeks planted was well
fitted to bear good fruit in later years.

Plato's definition of education as a "turning about of the soul" is very significant. It
implies a certain contempt for the belief that
education is mere acquisition of knowledge, as
though some "furniture of the mind" could be
bought from a dealer in such wares. It places
the emphasis on action, on the restless activity
of the mind which persists in living and growing whether we cultivate it or not. On this
point Plato is very insistent; he thinks there is
more hope for the quick-witted scoundrel than
for apathetic self-complacent mediocrity; he
knows that schools and lectures are only a
fraction of life, that the young life is not
bounded by time-tables, that in their play the
children are learning. This wonderful sense
for the vitality of the mind is Plato's great contribution to the psychology of education. It
contains implicitly all the details of his theory
of education: they are in fact no more than a
study of the forms of this activity. It is not

surprising, then, that Plato from the first struck the right note and selected for his theory the most fundamental points.

The first of these is the doctrine of mimēsis (μίμησις).[19] The English word imitation is not an adequate translation of this term, for it implies too easily the qualities of the " sedulous ape." Plato did not mean mimicry but spontaneous adoption of a pattern and consequent reproduction of that pattern in the expression which is life. Mimicry is conscious; the imitator knows that he is doing something different from his real life; but in mimesis there is no such dualism, for it is a trend of life which makes the character itself. The idea which Plato has in mind is derived from medicine, another phase of the persistent doctrine that a thing grows by what it feeds on. Plato knew the kind of teaching contained in the treatise on Airs, Waters, and Places. The Hippocratic schools deduced their hygiene from the cosmology of the physical philosophers, and the later philosophers repaid the debt by deducing their theory of mental development from the theory of good and bad states, health and disease. In both cases the crucial question is that of environment. As the Greek sanatorium was a temple of medicine set in places where the god of health might himself dwell, so the ideal home of the mind should be a place where all the surroundings perpetually create and sustain the health of the soul. Plato summed up this doctrine in a passage that can never be too often quoted either for its truth or its beauty.

" This being the case ought we to confine ourselves to superintending our poets and compelling them to impress on their productions the likeness of a good moral character, on pain of not composing among us; or ought we to extend our superintendence to the professors of every other craft as well and forbid them to impress those signs of an evil nature, of dissoluteness, of meanness, and of ungracefulness, either on the likenesses of living creatures, or on buildings, or on any other work of their hands; altogether interdicting such as cannot do otherwise from working in our city, that our guardians may not be reared amongst images of vice, as upon unwholesome pastures, culling much every day by little and little from many places, and feeding upon it, until they insensibly accumulate a large mass of evil in their inmost souls? Ought we not on the contrary, to seek out artists of another stamp, who by the power of genius can

trace out the nature of the fair and the grace-
ful, that our young men, dwelling as it were in a
healthful region, may drink in good from every
quarter, whence any emanation from noble
works may strike upon their eye or their ear,
like a gale wafting health from salubrious lands,
and win them imperceptibly from their earliest
childhood into resemblance, love, and harmony
with the true beauty of reason? "

From this passage it is clear that imitation
(mimesis) is a wide term which includes in
many cases what is now called " suggestion."
The importance of the external world consists
in its significance or meaning, and this ultimately shows that the values attached to natural objects are expressions of mental attitudes.
To express or to interpret is to create, and so
the suggestiveness of nature is really the power
by which it develops the mind which reacts
to it. In ordinary language the word suggestion is used in this sense quite correctly; when
a book is described as suggestive it is classed as
capable of developing in the reader some creative act of thought, expressing more than it
appears to say. A book which is " suggestive "
(for *suggestion* in this sense the Greek word is
ὑπόνοια) in the bad sense will illustrate the

principle even better, for " to the pure all things are pure " and therefore the evil suggestion is only effective in stimulating and developing minds that have acquired some tincture of vice. Plato includes in the sources of suggestion all the range of nature, but he distinguishes different kinds. As the child is predominantly a creature of feeling, natural objects affect it most intensely, though not in the form of reflective consciousness. This phase of Platonism has been reproduced with great fidelity by Wordsworth and no words could more accurately define Plato's hopes than the lines:

" *And beauty born of murmuring sound,*
  Shall pass into her face."

In the technical language of psychology the words imitation, suggestion, and sympathy are closely related. Imitation describes the behaviour which is suggested; suggestion indicates the subconscious character of the process, which is the secret of its power for good or evil; sympathy originally denoted the coincidence of feeling or communication of feeling which seems to occur spontaneously, as when an emotional state spreads through a group of per-

[83]

sons, though only one may know what the real trouble is. Professor MacDougall's phrase "sympathetic induction of emotion" is a good epitome of this doctrine, and, whatever may be the criticisms directed upon the implied theory, it conveniently and accurately describes the facts. With their gift for generalization the Stoics overworked the word sympathy and gave it a cosmic meaning. It must be admitted that they had some encouragement from Plato, for he, too, thought that there was some sensible affinity between the order of the Universe (Cosmos) and the order of a perfectly harmonious soul (κόσμιός τε καὶ θεῖος). But authors often need protection from their friends, and Plato might well object that what is good as an analogy may be objectionable as a dogma. For the Stoic writers made sympathy a mystical bond of unity between all parts of nature and so brought discredit on the term; their disciples increased the trouble by creating the fantastic doctrine of sympathetic magic, which was maintained down to the eighteenth century.

The original idea, much less pretentious and more useful, seems to have been restored to modern literature by Adam Smith. Smith's view of moral sentiments as "underived" led to the psychological doctrine that feelings are not products of calculation but occur, whenever the proper stimulus is provided, without being deduced from the concept of utility. He used the word " sympathy " for this immediate unreflective response.[20] The familiar example of the spectator in the theatre, whose hand reproduces the movement of the actor striking the blow, serves to show Smith's meaning. Adam Smith's theory of sympathy was important because it checked the tendency in the eighteenth century to explain all feelings as produced by rational calculation: also it united perception and action in one individual operation and so did away with the usual intermediate links. An unpremeditated response really shows the agent's character; it acts more rapidly and proceeds from a deeper stratum than second thoughts. In all these points Smith's theory serves as a good commentary on Plato's teaching. It bridges over the period from Plato to Gabriel Tarde in whom we find united all the elements of the tradition. Tarde called his book *The Laws of Imitation,* thus adopting the original term; the book itself was actually a study of suggestion and what the eighteenth century called " contagion of ideas "; finally, it was based on a rather superfluous type of cosmic theory according to which the rhythms and repetitions of the Universe were also uniformities dependent on a law of imitation. It is important to remember that theories of imitation or of repetition logically require a beginning and that this (*ex hypothesi*) is not under the same law. Provision must be made for invention as well as imitation, for beginning as well as repeating. Both Plato and Tarde seem to minimize the importance of this point, probably for the same reason. The democratic form of government in both ancient and modern times creates a fear of the weight of the masses, the actual pressure which is brought to bear on the individual by general attitudes of mind. Public opinion under the given conditions is liable to be little more than a wave of emotional unanimity, a form of conviction devoid of critical judgment. Since the striking force is in the masses, or in other words the emotions are the most dynamic element in all actions, the state and the individual are most often studied as organisms in need of control. Because of this attitude the literature of the subject is usually full of theories about the spread of ideas or the low mentality of crowds, while the origin of ideas and the character of the leaders receive less attention.

How well Plato and Aristotle understood the principles of crowd psychology can be shown by reference to two passages in their works. In the sixth book of the *Republic* Plato explains that the people are really the greatest sophists and most to blame for the corruption of youth. This they do " when they sit down together in large numbers in the assemblies or the law courts, or the theatres or camps, or any other place where crowds come together, and proceed with great noise and confusion to find fault with some of the things that are being said or done and to praise others, their fault-finding and their praise being equally extravagant, shouting and clapping their hands till the rocks and the place in which they are join with them and echo back redoubled the uproar of their condemnation and their praise. Amid such a scene where, think you, is a young man's heart? What private education will hold out and not be swamped by such a volume of condemnation and praise, and swept down stream wherever such a current takes it, till he call beautiful and ugly what they do, act as they do, and become like them? " In these words

Plato graphically presents the process which the psychologists of today call the "levelling effect" of crowds. From a different point of view Aristotle explains in the *Rhetoric* that mere reasoning is not likely to secure the assent of a body of people. To produce conviction or even gain a sympathetic hearing it is necessary first to create the right emotional state. Arguments are intended to produce conviction, but neither sincerity nor logical accuracy will achieve this result unless goodwill is first established. The successful pleader, in law or politics, must learn this art of exciting the right kind of emotion, for without a favourable attitude of mind the most cogent reasons will produce no effect. It is not surprising that a subtle politician like Francis Bacon valued this part of Aristotle most highly or that the courtly gentlemen of the Renaissance learned from it the secret art of winning favours from monarchs.

Plato seems to have thought that the practical sphere of education is always the production of normal citizens who "imitate" the human and divine laws of existence. The super-normal is not a product of this system; the system at its best can only make normal people capable of recognizing the great man when he comes. The case of Socrates seemed to show that on this point Athenian education had failed, and from Plato's time onward there are many indications that men were looking for a great statesman, a Saviour of the People, with the secret fear that he might come unrecognized or even be sacrificed to the ignorance and strong passions of the mob. This presentiment, though blind enough itself, now looks like a prophetic vision of the birth of Christianity. Since the supreme necessity for the subjects of the state is rational obedience, and the quality of the great ruler is also rational obedience to the higher laws of the Universe, Plato found the goal of education in this quality. The different stages on the road to this goal are marked by the peculiar characteristics of childhood, youth, and manhood. The broad description of these in psychological terms is that they represent the predominance of feelings, practical or applied knowledge, and reflective thought in sequence. These are the mental ages of man and each of them must be utilized in its turn.

Plato's treatment of political psychology is so broad and so untechnical in its manner that it either goes unnoticed or offends the modern reader. Yet nothing in Plato's works shows a

truer grasp of the principles of human behaviour. Plato knew that revolution is the end,
not the beginning, of a political change. The
beginning might be found in a song which the
young men learned to sing years ago. Plato
might have agreed with the man who said "Let
me make the nation's songs, and I care not who
makes their laws." He might have remembered
Tyrtaeus, and he would have understood the
political value of the Marseillaise; he knew
the orgiastic fury of the Phrygian tunes and
the steady beat of the Dorian march; today he
would be quoting the Puritans who were signifi-
cantly called "psalm-singers" and the Cava-
liers who were known by their lilts and rounde-
lays. Here Plato was on firm ground and
could generalize from a wide experience.
Music, in the narrower sense, was and still is a
powerful agent either for expressing or arous-
ing emotions; and every experience is a fresh
addition to the total structure of character. We
can hardly suppose that Plato knew anything
of the positive physiological effects of music.
The assertion has been made recently that the
vibrations of musical notes and chords have
such definite effects as relief of neuralgia; if
this is true, there would be a positive physio-

logical effect underlying the more general experiences of elation and depression which have always been recognized. The modern reader of Plato is too apt to think about music as part of a concert to which people listen with silent and motionless decorum. Plato himself would think first of music and motion as a unity in which there is one indivisible harmony. The dance is the best modern equivalent, but even there the conditions are rarely the same as those of primitive dances or the ancient ritualistic dances. The modern interest in eurhythmics is one of the most significant testimonies to the truth of Plato's teaching, which was itself no more than a conscious elaboration of elementary human experiences.

In the wider sense music includes literature, and this, too, Plato considers from a purely psychological standpoint. One of the most difficult problems in all educational schemes is that of making a transition from acceptance of existing standards to criticism of them. Literature, as understood by Plato, meant chiefly the embodied wisdom of the race as it appeared in poetry and folk-lore. The poets and the mythologists provided both worldly wisdom and the equivalent of what is called theology.

This is really no less than the general mental and spiritual atmosphere of life. Plato grasped the important fact that feelings are more pervasive and more permanent than ideas; the good and the beautiful can be distinguished from the scientifically true and, while truth in the sense of logical demonstration is not possible, there may yet be right and wrong attitudes. The modern enthusiasts for truth, who would do away with all fairy-stories and myths, seem to lack the psychological insight which Plato showed. Truth, according to Plato was to be judged first as truth in the inward parts, a right disposition of mind. The doctrine becomes almost pragmatic in its application, for Plato insists that we must believe such propositions as God is good, not because they are mathematically demonstrable but because they are formal principles of right action. The lack of the right disposition is described by Plato as the " genuine lie " or lie in the soul. This is not ignorance of fact but ignorance of principle and it constitutes a definite type of character, probably akin to that which Aristotle defines as incorrigibly corrupt (ἀκόλαστος).

In the *Republic* Plato works out the whole scheme of mental development and correlates with each stage the type of activity suitable to it. The names usually given to these stages are conjecture, belief, scientific demonstration, and dialectic.[21] The original terms are difficult to translate but their meaning can be conveyed in a brief description. The controlling idea is that mental life begins in a chaotic state of feelings and loose ideas, the *vaga experientia* of Spinoza or the "big buzzing blooming confusion" of William James. This is reduced to order by the needs of daily life, which provide the test of success or failure and give importance to the empirical knowledge of the means useful for desired ends. The practical knowledge of the workman, the rule of thumb methods and the traditional ways of doing things are now assimilated; the reason for all acts at this stage is the simple formula that "we always do it that way." Though it is crude and immature, this stage serves to lay a foundation for the higher stage of criticism and reflection. Scientific knowledge differs from the earlier stage in the fact that it abstracts the relations themselves from their concrete setting and sets its problems in terms of pure intellect. The type of abstract relations in this sense is the mathematical formula, and all experience goes to show that a grasp of such formulae is a crisis in mental development; it marked the transition from counting by pebbles to pure bookkeeping; it is still faced by every schoolboy when he begins arithmetic and still more when he passes on to algebra.

The knowledge of relations is the most important point in Plato's definition of intellectual knowledge. When the mind is developed the particular cases lose their importance as isolated facts and gain in compensation a new importance as cases of more general laws. There is room accordingly for infinite progress as more and more comprehensive generalizations open up and further relations can be discovered between the known sets of relations. A great amount of this is always relatively unpractical; as science goes ahead of traditional practice so philosophical speculation runs ahead of science, not as an irrelevant pursuit of different ends but as the progressive completion of the mental process through which the Universe may finally be known as a complete system of laws.

Plato's attempt to avoid separating knowledge into different departments leads him to speak at one and the same time about the physical world, the nature of knowledge, and the development of the mind. The objection naturally felt by the modern reader is that logic and psychology are hopelessly confused. But the situation is relieved by the fact that Plato really knew more about the mind than he knew about nature. His universe is conceived in a very anthropomorphic fashion as having the unity which belongs to the mind. When he asserts that all parts of the body (as we should say, the nervous system) are drawn up in the head and subordinated to the ruling part, his statements are more correct than his reasons for making them. The psychology is made more plausible by being harmonized with the cosmology; but it can stand by itself, and as such it is a perfectly reasonable analysis. Its guiding principle is the simple rule of progress from plurality to unity, from incoherence to coherence, from disintegration to integration. A more empirical method would have paid less attention to the ideal type of completely integrated personality; but the social and political interest, the desire to assist the production of the highest type of citizen and especially of the legislator who should interpret to man the ways of God, explains this emphasis and accounts for the limitations of the treatment.

2. SOCIETY AND POLITICS

THE unity of Greek life in the days of the City State is reflected in the unity of their political theory. The individual and the community are two aspects of one reality; as Plato stated it, the community is the individual writ large. It was natural for the Greek to look for an explanation of social unity in some characteristic of the mind; for unity and obligation were not imposed from outside but grew up as the developed consciousness of social relations. In modern times this has emerged again as the final question; politics has been allied with sociology and history has been described as fundamentally a psychological subject. While Plato is most interested in the process of making good citizens, he is also interested in the problem of social and political stability. This he rightly treats as a problem in social psychology.

The doctrine of Eros which was so important for individual psychology (v. p. 58) now becomes the basis of social psychology. Through the driving force of Eros we reach the goal of existence. This word Eros, like the word Justice, has a peculiar richness of content; it is a name for a transcendental principle which is manifested in different ways according to the material in which it operates. If we are speaking of the inorganic we may call it physical attraction; if we are speaking of the organic, we may call it assimilation; if we are speaking of conscious organisms we may call it a feeling of attraction, a desire, or simply Love. Plato's use of this term in treating the upward movement of the created to the uncreated or eternal, is a fine flight of imagination which we propose to ignore at the present moment; its brilliance has obscured too much the fact that at bottom this is a scientific interpretation of society as an inevitable natural outcome of laws which man neither makes nor unmakes. The neglect of the less poetic aspects can hardly be astonishing; Plato himself submerges them; generations of readers before and after Shelley have revelled in the spacious romanticism of dialogues like the *Symposium;* only the new interests which have emerged in modern sociology could suffice to bring the less conspicuous details into notice. Yet they are there for a purpose and when properly understood they will be properly judged.

Both Plato and Aristotle seem to find a starting point in a quotation from Empedocles. There the word used is not ἔρως (*Eros*), but the more significant term στοργή (*storgē*). The relation of these two terms is like that between δικαιοσύνη and μοῖρα. In each case the former term has been specialized and only faintly recalls the ruder days of primitive culture; the latter term, on the contrary, seems filled with a primaeval intensity. Law and justice are works of reason beginning from the primitive dividing up of things; love and friendship are similarly works of reason which began from a primitive elemental passion. Empedocles was no metaphysician in the Aristotelian sense; he was a physiologist, an expert in the ways of nature. For him there was no yearning of the soul after divine beauty; the plain facts of chemical affinities and compatible temperaments were all he saw in his world of elements and mixtures. That was the strong positivism of his century — the positivism of the medical schools. It lives now as it lived then. While the new social science was growing up about 1840, the greatest edition of Hippocrates ever produced by a single hand was made by Littré, the modern positivist's tribute to his Greek master. If we now turn to the

Symposium we shall find a careful arrangement of the data. The first speaker's point is that love is the root of honour and dishonour; it is the sensibility or sensitiveness which makes us social creatures in so far as that involves caring about other people's opinions and feelings. This Love, of which the poets sang, is the eldest of the gods; before it, there was nothing, and it had no parents; it is, in other words, the most fundamental thing we can imagine. The next speakers rather drift away from this notion. They show us Love developed into conscious desire, narrowed, made personal, badly understood and spoiled by its union with intellects not adequate to its high estate. The speakers are really a little drunk and inclined to exhibit in themselves the shallow emotions of a civilized dinner party. Aristophanes, who should come next, is temporarily incapacitated and the medical man, Eryximachus, is substituted. This brings us back to the impersonal viewpoint, the scientific spirit which would treat love as somehow a matter of cosmic harmony, and abolish the distinction between goodness and badness in the sphere of passions, in favour of a distinction between health and disease. Aristophanes having now recovered, his substitute is withdrawn; obviously he is only let in to give us a hint and withdrawn because Plato does not intend to develop that theme. Instead we are permitted to hear Alcibiades, who being drunk, is free of speech; finally we hear Socrates, who is made almost unintelligible by excess of inspiration. In sum, these speakers show us that the evolution of man from primitive societies up to the highest, can be written in terms of the gregarious instincts and their relation to reason. The genesis and the final cause of society are one and the same; it begins from the desire for complete self-realization, and it is justified because it alone can provide the circumstances under which the self realizes its power of thought and expression.

What Plato describes so broadly in the *Symposium* is again stated by Aristotle in the *Nicomachean Ethics*. There the subject is treated as a scientific account of human relations, a theory of society. We are introduced in the *Ethics* to a point of view which is more profound than the issues of politics or economics; while they deal with the organization of the objective life of the state, the *Ethics* deals with the human instincts out of which all fellowship grows. Aristotle proposes to show how the raw material of instincts and impulses becomes socialized. As usual, the treatment of the subject lacks the picturesque qualities of the Platonic method, but it is in many ways equal to the earlier outline. In the third and fourth books of the *Ethics* the virtues are carefully arranged so as to show in what sense they are forms of primary instincts. The first two are courage and temperance. Courage comes first because it is rooted in the fundamental will to live, in the ferocity of the animal that defends itself and its young, in the elemental quality of pugnacity. Temperance is next, because hunger and thirst and sexual desire are the primary somatic impulses: without these there could not be life and without control of these there could be no good life. Another level is reached when human development creates a different class of objects — property, honour, and the ends of rational desire. Here we find different instincts emerging, such as acquisitiveness and ambition, which also require to be trimmed and adjusted to the proper degree of moderation. Finally society itself creates a set of relations which depend on the interaction between minds, the sense of honour, respect for truth, and refinement of humour which make ideal companionship.

If Aristotle had announced that he would write a treatise on the evolution of civilized man, the skill and insight of these passages would not have been so constantly overlooked. Aristotle's sense for development is so strong that he seems to be unconscious of any effort to prove evolution; he is content to arrange the stages in their natural order and leave them to produce conviction. In the third and fourth books of the *Ethics*, the human being is shown as a creature " neither beast nor god," but literally an animal fit for civilized life. The description is purely psychological and consists in showing how the natural endowment of man provides the material for its expansion and refinement. In the eighth and ninth books the same topic is considered from the point of view of complete development; the conditions of social life are then analyzed in terms of psychological factors. To do this Aristotle goes back to the primitive sense of kinship, the dumb craving for companionship — $\sigma\tau o\rho\gamma\dot{\eta}$. This is the natural root of parental affection, and so accounts for the place which the family holds in the evolution of society. But reason is the highest level of human evolution, and as the purely emotional impulse, the elemental sense of kinship, widens out into community of purpose, it becomes Friendship ($\phi\iota\lambda\iota a$).

There seems to be no Anglo-Saxon equivalent to this use of $\phi\iota\lambda\iota a$; friendship is only a make-shift. To understand its meaning we must consider the different relations which it describes. In the case of father and son it is parental affection; in the case of husband and wife it is conjugal affection, a complex of tenderness, authority, and respect; in the case of a ruler it is the benevolence which tempers authority, making the ruler also the father of his people. The idea of society as a psychological unity in which all this variety of " friendship " was nourished and preserved, never quite disappeared from western thought. The Stoics did not understand it because for them government was cosmic and remote; but the Epicureans preserved it in their idea of voluntary associations. In modern times, whenever Communistic or any other anti-monarchical movements have been in vogue, the same tendency has been revived. Echoing the sentiments of Plato and endorsing the theory of Aristotle, men then adopt the term " brother " to signify that the only political obligation they acknowledge is derived from a consciousness of kinship.

In the eighth book of the *Republic* Plato attempted an explanation of the ways in which social transformations are caused. He traces the influences which from generation to generation bring about the transformation of values. The great problem of social philosophy is to combine might with right. What actually brings about the decline and fall of a community is the tendency of the rising generation to feel that righteousness does not involve power, that goodness is not as desirable as success. Plato's astonishingly keen observation of the mental attitudes which finally become social and political characteristics is one of the few attempts ever made to apply psychology to political history and deserves to be carefully studied. Writing in the second century B.C. Polybius (*Histories*, vi. 5) refers to the Platonic theory of political changes and gives a summary of it so far as he supposes it " to fall within the scope of a practical history and the intelligence of ordinary people." In this summary Polybius shows a remarkable sense for the psychological factors. Assuming that human history were to begin again, he attributes the first development to herd-instinct; in the herd the aggressive qualities would cause some to become leaders; this would be despotism, modified at a later time to kingship. In this stage government is qualified by morality; morality is the instinctive tendency to feel gratitude for parental care, to resent ingratitude, to support those who deserve rewards and punish by disapproval those who ignore these rights. Clearly Polybius understood what we still call the social sentiments and would have agreed with Adam Smith's two doctrines, that sympathy is a principle of action and that society moderates the sentiments of individuals as an " impartial spectator."

3. ABNORMAL STATES

IN modern psychology the study of the abnormal types of mental activity occupies a large place. It is interesting to see how far the ancient writers dealt with this part of the subject.

In the earliest writers the idea of normal activity is so inadequately defined that the abnormal does not stand out clearly. The ideal type is the clear intellect and divergences from this are indicated as states of ignorance. These divergences are regarded with some contempt as merely lower classes of intellect. In the Homeric period there is clearly a high valuation of practical shrewdness and the sensible man stands out in contrast to the incapable man who has no power to outwit his enemies or successfully carry out his designs. In the Pre-Socratic period this appears as a distinct doctrine of the relation between higher and lower faculties. The excellence of the highest type of mind is presented at this stage as consisting primarily in the power of using the reason. To remain at the level of the senses is to suffer delusion and dwell in a region of obscurity. But so far there is nothing beyond a distinction in degrees of ability. Plato's treatment of the soul shows a continuance of this tradition with a tendency to make the distinction of greater and less ability into a distinction of goodness and badness. This change introduces a new feature, for now we find that the disturbing factor is desire, and consequently there is an indistinct suggestion that the basis of mental excellence is the control of passions.[22] This is a view which invites comparison with the modern treatment of morbid psychological states. For the essential element in many diseases of the mind is a want of balance due to the tension of diverging impulses. A modern writer treats this tension as a relation between inherent impulses and acquired forms of restraint. The Greek formulates this condition as a conflict between desire and reason, but the difference in meaning is not great. In Plato there is distinct recognition of this inner tension and its results. In the *Republic* the passion of love is described as a " frantic and savage monster "; the reason is only freed from the strain of controlling this passion when age brings "profound repose and freedom from this and other passions." In the eighth and ninth books of the *Republic* Plato gives an elaborate account of the way in which abnormal types are developed through faulty education or circumstances; the point maintained throughout is that the balance of mind is upset by the extreme development of some inherent tendency. At the close of the ninth book a vivid description is given of the composite nature of man. Plato asks the hearer to mould " the form of a motley many-headed monster, furnished with a ring of heads of tame and wild animals, which he can produce by turns in every instance out of himself " ; then, secondly, the form of a lion and, thirdly, the form of a man. These are then combined into one and we have man as he is, externally one but internally a plurality of forces. The same idea is stated less allegorically in the *Laws* (644) where man is said to be in some sense a puppet of the Gods; what the ultimate purpose of life is we cannot know, but we know that "the affections in us are like cords and strings which pull us different and opposite ways"; it is our duty to pull the cord of reason. This, Plato says, is the practical meaning of the expression "superior or inferior to a man's self."

On this basis Plato is able to treat the criminal mind in a way that has some historical interest. The criminal is for Plato primarily an object of pity; the doctrine that vice is ignorance is practically a declaration that crime is disease. This aspect is most clearly stated in the *Laws* (854), where Plato anticipates that some citizens will prove hard-hearted and resist the gentle appeal of words in the law. He takes the case of robbing temples; no good citizen will catch such an infection, but servants and others might be led astray, by "suggestion." Such a crime denotes an incurable state; a tormenting desire drives the man, day and night, to rob a temple; we can do nothing except

explain to the victim that this is not a human
or divine affliction, but a madness begotten in
men by ancient and unexpiated crimes; we must
exhort him in these hours of temptation to call
upon his Gods, seek the company of the good,
hear and repeat the saying that every man
must honour the right. Finally, if nothing
avails to check the criminal tendency, the person should depart from this life.

This passage explains in a remarkable way
the character of those obsessions that produce
crimes; the power of suggestion in causing and
curing crime is clearly indicated; and, in a curious way, the criminal is described as dispas-
sionately renouncing his hopeless " lower nature." Modern psychology recognizes that
there is sometimes this dualism; more frequently the obsession leaves no room for such
self-condemnation. The Greek belief, that the
soul dwelt in the body, tends to make this self-
condemnation appear natural; the man, as soul,
condemns himself, as agent. Here we see how
ancient theory failed through lack of knowledge; with no idea of brain or nerves, little
could be expected. The state of total obsession
is called by Plato the darkness of the soul, a
lie in the soul, an ultimate corruption of the

moral powers (v. p. 92). This is usually the extreme type of ignorance, or amentia, and is a fruitful source of crime. The causes of crime are enumerated as passion, pleasure, and ignorance. These work in different ways; passion sweeps the man along, pleasure sophisticates his reasoning, ignorance blinds his soul. By ignorance Plato does not mean a failure to know some isolated fact, unless he expressly assigns it that meaning; ignorance is a name for that condition of the soul in which there is a permanent deficiency of the moral sense, a condition akin to what might be called today atrophy of the moral consciousness. This " ignorance " is in reality loss of the power to estimate values, and the word has just the elusive character which belongs to all terms used to express loss of " the will to be good." Ignorance in this sense is not regarded as connate but as the result of a certain kind of conduct; it therefore fails to include hereditary lack of moral insight; and the Greeks tended to think of crime as going on from generation to generation but *not* by physical heredity; it is one eternal wrath that outlives each generation and persecutes its successor. In this way the Greeks missed the problem which heredity makes acute, namely personal responsibility for crime; there is a tendency to limit the question to the life of the individual, a standpoint which is practically valuable but theoretically too narrow in outlook. The question of individual treatment is adequately discussed. The laws give external support to morality; but the real cure for immorality is the cultivation of three principles — piety, love of honour, and love of beauty in the soul; in other words religion, society, and art are the effective antidotes to mental degradation and spiritual lawlessness.

Between the imaginations of a diseased mind and the phenomena of normal dreams there is no great difference; both imply a decrease in the power of centralization and control. The best appendix to Plato's account of the criminal mind is his treatment of dreams. Having seen that the normal waking state is characterized by a high degree of control (self-control or suppression of desire) he is able to group the abnormal states together as types of decentralization or loss of control, and dreams furnish an analogy. The doctrine is clearly summed up in the *Republic*.[23] There we are told that the waking state is one of restraint; in sleep this rational control is released and the imagination, a sensuous faculty, runs riot and pictures all those excesses of passion which the desires suggest but which habits of restraint have kept in abeyance at other times.

In these passages we see how conscious Plato was of the complexity of human nature. He had learned the science of his contemporaries and grasped the idea that human progress could be judged by the degree to which man could employ the higher faculties and "let the ape and tiger die." The same fundamental doctrine is expressed in his idea of Eros (v. p. 97), as having a lower and a higher form. The sensuous passion coexists with the loftier and purer passion and men waver between "bursts of great heart and slips in sensual mire." These broad generalizations were not supported by any direct study of abnormal types. To some extent the Greek drama had become a study of psychological types. An Oedipus or a Phaedra was presented as an instance of morbid states; Orestes was an example of mental derangement due to terrible experiences; but all this is distinctively objective in method and therefore misses the special subjective analysis required to make it a psychological study. Poets, philosophers, and men of science were halting between two opinions; magic was decaying and with it the belief in external agencies as causes of disease in mind or body, but the belief was by no means dead. The most significant case for our purposes is that of inspiration or enthusiasm, and it is highly instructive to see how these abnormal states are treated.

It is necessary here to recall the fact that Greek thought regarded the soul as dual, and considerable confusion arises from this dualism. In any abnormal state either the higher or the lower part may attain an exceptional activity. Crime and some dream-states belong to the class of states in which the lower part is excessively active; but at the same time a dream-state is one in which the higher part is set at liberty, so that it attains a pure activity at such times and may become prophetic. Here there is obvious confusion between several points of view, depending largely on the fact that the duality of conduct is derived from a distinction between soul and body, and then refunded as a distinction between reason and desire within the soul. The problems involved in this became apparent when other excessive activities were discussed. The term madness (*mania*, μανία) covers all types of excessive action in which the individual develops powers above his normal level. The inspiration of the rhapsodist, of the poet, and of the seer are all "mania." Plato could find no place for those in his psychology; they were not morbid states of desire, nor activities of reason, and yet they were undeniable facts and in a sense superhuman; so he took the natural course and left this class by itself. The term "enthusiasm," denoting the indwelling of a god, served as a name for creative imagination and religious mania. Mental exaltation of this kind was a mystery to the Greek; he was aware that music could induce the state and also counteract the symptoms; he understood that it was in some degree pathological but a sense of its utility in art and of its function in divination prevented him from arriving at any but a mystical conception of its nature.

Aristotle has little to say on this subject and the doctrine of inspiration becomes the peculiar property of the Platonizing theorists. Of these the most conspicuous were Plutarch, Plotinus, and Augustine. Aristotle seems to have approached the subject along the lines of scientific classification. He distinguishes between con-

nate unnatural tendencies and acquired or morbid propensities. The former belong to the
class called bestial and include habits which
are no longer found among civilized people.
The latter are various habits or mental states
which result from diseases, such as tearing the
hair or biting the nails. Aristotle also quotes as
instances the practice of eating ashes or earth
and adds sexual irregularities as a general class.
It is obvious from this list that some definite
ideas about mental diseases and abnormal psychology were at least on the way to being
formed and recorded. The Hippocratic school
had already swept away the myth of the
"sacred disease": epilepsy was recognized as
a disease and not a supernatural visitation; it is
difficult to tell from the scattered suggestions
found in Aristotle how much was actually
known but in all probability the range of information was not great.

The idea of a distinction between normal and
abnormal activities is connected in Greek
thought with the idea of a correct and incor-
rect mixture of the four humours. The mixture
of the humours constitutes the type physically
and mentally. This is the doctrine of temperaments which deserves honourable mention

as one of the most persistent ideas in the whole range of human thought. It seems to have originated in the work of a man called Polybus and was a feature of the Sicilian school of medicine as represented by Empedocles. The original terms are still in common use and people are popularly classed as sanguine, phlegmatic, choleric, or melancholic. In very recent times new classifications have been devised on different principles, but the basic idea of the temperament remains unchanged. Whether right or wrong in the details of his physiology, the Greek set a good example in determining a temperament by the total physical and mental characteristics, and this principle has been consistently followed ever since. The humours have given place to nerves and glands, but the essential point in theories of temperament is still the "law of mixture," now called physiological balance.

IV. HELLENISTIC THOUGHT

WHEN we leave the works of Plato and Aristotle we become painfully conscious that the literature of ancient philosophy can offer us only an elaborate but inferior appendix. It is usual to say that the Hellenistic Age was an age of religion. There is no real justification for this. It was equally an age of science and literature. The most appropriate title would be the age of specialization, for that phrase expresses the actual facts and also explains why the period seems to become peculiarly religious. Though the psychology of this period is scientifically inferior, the period itself is very important on account of the fact that it becomes Roman as well as Greek, and through the persistence of its Latin terminology has influenced all subsequent writers.

The schools of the Graeco-Roman world were not well defined. For convenience of exposition we may regard the Stoic tradition, with all its variations, as the dominant factor between the years 322 B.C. and A.D. 430, from Aristotle to Augustine. This Stoic tradition went through several phases and ultimately lost its original distinctive features, but we shall ignore all these details and consider only the ideas which were carried down the stream to later centuries. The scientific influences which became dominant in this period destroyed the Greek sense for limits; that "progress to infinity" which Aristotle regarded as mere loss of control, became in this age a triumphant expansion from the *Polis* to the *Cosmos,* from the knowable to the unknowable. The Platonic tradition, represented by the keen logic of the sceptical Carneades, could refute the pretensions of the Stoics but could not destroy their appeal to human emotions; the only result was to make Stoicism less coherent and precipitate the age of eclecticism. Mathematics and the special sciences went their own way and left great legacies, such as the geometry of Euclid, the mechanics of Archimedes, the astronomy of Aristarchus, the botany of Theophrastus, the anatomy of Erasistratus, and the final achievements of Ptolemy and Galen. This specialization seemed to have little bearing on the nature and the destiny of the soul. The persistent demand for some solution of these problems led to speculations of the most unregulated kind and produced a chaos of superstitions about spirits and astral realms from which the human race derived all the inspiration it needed for the propagation of witchcraft and magic. From this confused mass of doctrines it is necessary to select the few points that have proved significant in the history of psychological theories.

The Stoic influence can be shown by tracing the variations in the use of certain cardinal terms. *Pneuma*, for example, is a significant word. It persists among the medical writers as a name for the animal spirits (v. p. 25) and represents the material or physiological basis of mental activity. Among speculative writers it becomes the name of an all pervading ether, present alike in man and the Universe, therefore a link between the individual and the Cosmos. Similarly *Logos*, (λόγος), a term for the rational functions of the pneuma, ceases to be merely speech or reasoning as it appeared in the earlier Greek writings; it becomes a cosmic Reason in which man has a share during his corporeal life and with which he may achieve hereafter eternal harmony and union. If the idea of Reason thus became less definite, it became at the same time more widespread and more comprehensive. This was shown particularly in the evolution of the ideas of instinct and conscience.

The classical writers did not develop any theory of the mind of animals. Aristotle is prepared to call animals " rational " in the sense that they can be habituated to make rational responses, and in this respect he thinks that animals and children are much alike; they are in a pre-rational state, potentially rational; animals do not progress beyond this stage, but children develop into completely rational beings. In one remarkable passage Aristotle decides that animals are very nearly machines; he anticipates with striking similarity the attitude of Descartes, though the saving clause is added which makes sensations and images factors in the production of movements. The passage in the *De Motu Animalium* runs thus: [24]

" The movements of animals may be compared with those of automatic puppets, which are set going on the occasion of a tiny movement; the levers are released and strike the twisted strings against one another; or with the toy waggon. . . . Animals have parts of a similar kind, their organs, the sinewy tendons to wit and the bones; the bones are like the wooden levers in the automaton, and the iron; the tendons are like the strings, for when these are tightened or released movement begins." The only difference between such a pure mechanism and an animal is that in the animal changes are qualitative; the parts become larger by warmth and smaller by cold. Sensations, imaginations, and ideas act in this way; for this reason " we shudder and are frightened at a mere idea."

The Stoics were carried by their general theory of life far beyond this cautious estimate. They found in the successful adaptation of the animal to its environment a source of perpetual wonder. The only solution was to make the Logos responsible. Indwelling in the animal and working, as we should say, unconsciously, it directed all the movements of animals to the attainment of the more important ends. Cicero, who seems to have taken a benevolent delight in dwelling on these marvels of Providence, is lavish in his description of the first natural objects (*prima naturalia*) and in his assurance that the animals were endowed with the necessary powers to compass all the means of self-preservation. Whatever may be the shortcomings of the method, its results were destined to last through all the literature of the West and to go unchallenged until the last few years. The Logos in the animal organism was an infallible urge or desire to the right action at the right time. Since it thus pricked the animal it was called by the Romans the "instinctus," a word which suggests the prick of the goad and the blind forward plunge of the animal thus manipulated by an all-powerful and all-wise driver. Thus instinct is a mode of behaviour which serves a useful purpose without previous knowledge of the end; and this description remains the most natural and popular interpretation of the facts. It is, however, full of difficulties and these were soon discovered. Since knowledge of the end was in any case only a luxury and man was himself only the vehicle of a divine purpose, there was no basis for distinguishing between reason and instinct except so far as reflection on the primitive impulses made them less certain and less useful. In that case the usual valuation would be reversed; the uncorrupted instincts would be more natural, and therefore more divine, than the turgid thinking of sophisticated mankind. This strain has often reappeared in literature. Those who in-

dulge vain fancies about the simple life or the
simple faith, some exponents of the *élan vital*,
and adherents of animal faith as contrasted
with scepticism, are all witnesses to the en-
chantment of this theory. It lulled suspicion
to sleep and disarmed criticism. Consequently
animal stories became more and more defiant of
probability; to a supernatural power like instinct all things must be possible. Plutarch of
Chaeronea has a profound belief in the sagacity
of animals; Pliny is prepared to register any
new report of their wisdom, foresight, and
piety; the Alexandrians ran amok in the
jungles of their own natural history; and the
miserable fatuity of the *Physiologus* and the
later *Bestiaries* completed the descent to ignorance.

Judged by the standards of popularity and
longevity, conscience must be considered one
of the greatest discoveries of all time. It
might almost be called an invention; like the
great scientific hypotheses it was invented
rather than discovered. The classical schools
had not needed this concept. There was nothing mysterious about their morality; a man
could know what was expected of him and do it
or not do it; he could reap praise or blame and

he could feel shame or self-satisfaction; it was all above board and the game was played according to the rules. Here and there something a little uncanny is suspected. One person claims to have a " daimon " that does wonders; another is talking about unwritten laws; the poets, who are always inclined to be oracular, annually produce a crop of rather depressing examples of dooms and repentances; the Orphics are continually hinting at something called purity of heart, but they are notorious quacks and apparently have something to sell. Thus the plain man would reflect on the course of life and be at rest. But not so the Stoic. In an age of loose morality, with no strict allegiance to any group, cosmopolitan and therefore *déraciné,* the Stoic was haunted by the intangible fear of deadly sin. He said to himself in his own way what the Hebrew had said before: though I make my bed in Hell, thou art there. The Stoic had no knowledge of the modern solution; it did not occur to him to accuse society of manufacturing conscience, nor would he have been satisfied with the shallowness of the doctrine that it was only " fear of the other fellow." He would not even regard it as " an accumulated mass of feeling " with

John Stuart Mill, or let it go as an emotion. With far deeper psychological insight the Stoic seized the essential point. Whatever its origin, its nature is simple; it is the state of mind which marks the fact that a man has come unto himself. Apart from all question of detection or punishment, the Stoic sees in conscience the immediate conviction of sin. The Greeks called it συνείδησις, *syneidesis,* or *synteresis;* the Romans translated the word literally into *conscientia,* and so began the history of a notable idea.

The theological development of this topic is not within the scope of this book, but the independent reality of this mental state deserves some comment. The Stoics and their successors did not confuse conscience with knowledge of commandments; they did not attempt to prove that particular dogmas were revealed to man through the acts of a faculty called conscience. As Paul understood it or Joseph Butler, conscience was primarily consciousness at the level of moral distinctions; it was in fact moral sanity, in the sense in which the modern alienist has argued for a recognition of moral sanity and insanity. The Logos dwells in man and is its own witness; the conscience, void of offence, cannot be convicted or condemned; though the law makes him a martyr to his cause, the inner light burns inextinguishably. Among modern people the Russians apparently preserve this mentality. Dostoievski is witness to the fact that the criminal in Russia often feels acutely the fact that he has sinned against humanity; though he evades the law he cannot evade himself, and the craving for reconciliation and atonement finally leads him to claim his punishment. The subject is enticing but must not be developed here; it is enough to indicate in this connection that in creating the idea of conscience the Stoics were not committing themselves to all the later vagaries of doctrine but expressing what may well be regarded as one of the most characteristic and fundamental forms of human behaviour.

Along with instinct and conscience the doctrine of innate ideas deserves mention, if only to establish its good and bad qualities. The Stoics were firm believers in the doctrine that knowledge is acquired during the natural life by way of sense-experiences. They compare the mind to a sheet of clean paper ready for writing, or to a tablet of wax unmarked by the stylus. There are then no innate ideas; man comes into the world with no furniture of the mind, perhaps even without a mind; for some writers postponed the advent of " reason " till the seventh or the tenth year. Innate ideas were in fact an invention of the later Middle Ages, when religious fervour generated the belief that all men are endowed at birth with at least a knowledge of God and the Ten Commandments. John Locke's attack on innate ideas was little more than a local skirmish; there was no major battle in progress and there was no intention of combating Platonism or Stoicism. The tradition that Plato taught a doctrine of innate ideas and that empiricism delivered mankind from this incubus, is a curious aberration of the historians. But there was some ground for it and it is worth while to rehearse the evidence.

In the days of Plato the current views of sensation and sense-experience seemed likely to eliminate reason altogether from the life of man. Against this Plato protested that the senses were instruments by which the mind acted, not funnels down which " sensations " could be poured (v. p. 40). The activity of the mind, thus affirmed, became a problem; some parts of the activity might be wholly independent of the senses; other parts would be employed in organizing sense-material. Plato's position can be defined negatively; he did not believe that the *acts* of the mind could be explained by description of its *contents*. Teaching cannot supply the power to learn; the intelligence is either present or not present; those objects which are only intelligible and have no spatial existence, depend on the connate powers, as for example the proposition " The whole is greater than the part." In all cases of really elementary facts, we can only rely on the person's ability to grasp the meaning; to that extent something is innate. Aristotle left the question very much in the same position; the intellect cannot be " derived." The Stoics did not propose to let the matter rest in so ambiguous a form. In harmony with their ideas about the indwelling Pneuma and the Logos, they sought for " common notions " which would be the same for all, an inevitable activity of Reason itself. This is practically equivalent to distinguishing intelligence from information; particular knowledge is acquired information, but general knowledge and the power to see distinctions is truly innate to the soul. When modern philosophy ran riot in empiricism and assumed (in haste) that experience could only be an operation of the sense, the same problem was revived; how could the " eye of the soul " be the product of its own acts of vision? In the Stoic revival of the seventeenth century Descartes found a convenient standpoint; he could make the soul independent of the bodily currents or nerve-impulses, and yet retain the utility of general ideas by making " innate ideas " no more than natural powers of discrimination and comprehension. The traditional dispute about innate and acquired ideas was really the historical form of the present discussion about the relation of act to content.

While the Stoics of the earlier period were inclined to elaboration and refinement of theories, the writers of the Roman school aimed to be severely practical. This characteristic is well illustrated by the treatment of memory. As the Sophists in Greece prepared young men for practical success in political life, so the schools of oratory among the Romans were the training grounds of the young men who hoped to make their mark in Roman politics. The " orator " is in fact the cultivated gentleman concerned with affairs of state; he must have enough knowledge to make a good speech, and of course he must be able to remember the right thing at the right time. Memory is therefore a topic of practical interest, and as such it is treated. Very little observation and some empirical psychology served to reveal the right principles. As examples of the results we may take the discourses of Cicero and Quintilian, both discussing the making of "orators." Apparently Simonides of Ceos was the traditional inventor of memory-systems; to him Cicero does homage, recounting the story of the banquet at which the guests were killed and how Simonides recalled each one by reproducing the order in which they had been arranged at table. This leads on to some very sound advice about associating words and ideas with places or with marks on the wax tablet; in short, Cicero explains quite adequately the use of visualization for recollection. Quintilian (A.D. 35–c. 95) follows the same tradition with more elaboration.[25] He commends the association of events with places, and similarly ideas of things; we might remember in proper order a set of words by putting them in places, e.g., table in the vestibule, couch in the hall and so forth. Quintilian adds that "perhaps those were assisted by this method who, at the close of an auction,

[130]

could specify what had been sold to each buyer." But in the matter of speech-making Quintilian rightly feels that this is not a good method; the flow of words will be broken by attempts to recall the associated symbols; the Roman, in fact, had already met with the difficulty of remembering the symbols adopted as reminders of something else. Quintilian's "simpler way" is to break up the speech into parts and learn each part separately; the speech should be learned from the tablets on which it was written, as the visual impression assists recollection; also things should be repeated aloud for then we listen to ourselves and so at the same time say the words and hear them. Other points are discussed but need not be repeated here; it is enough to produce this evidence of the development of *memoria technica* among the ancients. Nothing has been produced since Quintilian's days which would greatly improve or amplify his remarks. The psychology of education in modern times undertakes to do Quintilian's work, and agrees or disagrees about the relative merits of learning by parts, learning the whole, repeating with intervals and all the other experimental possibilities. For the public, Pelmanism and other

similar systems are the antidotes for forget-
fulness, and succeed by very similar methods.
Quintilian's final decision, that the only and
great art of memory is exercise and labour, is
too hard a doctrine for human acceptance. Men
still look for some magic which will convert for-
getfulness into memory. Perhaps Simonides
had anticipated our modern magicians by find-
ing a way to make men work without discovering the quantity of their own labours.

As the Stoic doctrine progressed it became
more and more disconnected and sporadic. The
original attempt to make soul and body aspects
rather than parts of the organism, proved un-
successful. Poseidonius went back to undis-
guised dualism in the interests of ethical and
religious aspirations. Ethical teachers preferred the Platonic view of a struggle between
the higher and the lower self. Religious dev-
otees required a scheme which led naturally
to a separation of the soul from the body and
provided a basis for a doctrine of the after-life.
The consequence was chaos. Stoicism became
Platonism and Platonism became a collection
of bastard doctrines which went under the
vague pseudonym of Neo-Pythagoreanism.
The fine insight which the early Stoics showed

was thus lost. At Alexandria science went its own way and evaded the orgy of religious enthusiasm which swept across Asia toward Rome. At the beginning of the Christian era Ptolemy created the astronomical system which goes by his name; Galen a little later summed up the work of the ancient world in anatomy and medicine. One final effort was made to interpret life and mind before the end came and that was the work of Plotinus.

Between 500 B.C. and A.D. 200 the ancient world presents a specimen of every known kind of psychological enquiry. The earliest stage furnishes scientific or objective accounts of perception and thought. From Socrates onward we find this supplemented by introspective and analytical work, with corollaries touching on immortality and kindred subjects. Aristotle carries this progress to its highest point in a mixed presentation of medical, biological, and philosophical doctrines. Even experiment is not wholly neglected, for the famous experiment of holding a marble between crossed fingers is ascribed to Aristotle. The spiritual or mystical vein is found in Plato and zealously worked by some of the later writers, especially by the Christian Platonists of Alexandria (*c.* A.D. 200). At the end of this long development comes Plotinus, a pupil of the Alexandrian school but a resident in Rome, himself the union of the two great traditions of his age and a worthy exponent of a Platonism which had been so continuously damaged and repaired that it might well take a new lease of life as Neo-Platonism.

So far as concerns psychological teaching the views of Plotinus can be stated briefly and clearly. They constitute the purest form of psychology which the ancient world produced. This was not a revolution; it was a normal, logical development. The stages may be summed up as follows. First, Plato protested against the crude notion that sensation was a kind of injection of knowledge. Aristotle supported this protest by eliminating the " impression " as something imported from without; in its place he put a significant change of state, a discrimination between modes of feeling. The Stoics followed with a theory that had no real place for impressions and could only formally distinguish between active and passive conditions of the pneuma. How or why a movement of this ethereal substance should be cognitive was not explained; the natural conclusion was to omit everything except the immediacy of experience. This becomes the standpoint of Plotinus. Its acceptance was a bold stroke and would have been futile if the writer had not known his ground so well or been so great a master of logical exposition.

There often comes a point in the progress of thought when the mass of material breaks down under its own weight. The genius sees how to reconstruct the scheme with greater simplicity: a Copernicus comes to the rescue. In the case of Plotinus the principle of simplicity required complete change of direction. Instead of bringing in experiences from without, the experience as it is in the mind will be the starting point and the problem to solve is the problem of outward projection. We must take this method seriously and apply it honestly. First we accept the proposition that the body is in the soul, contradicting the Platonizing Pythagoreans who say the soul is in the body. Religion may rebel against science and put an immortal soul in a mortal body; but that is bad science and primitive religion; our Neo-Platonist is not of that kind, and he will refuse both dogmas. His reason is that every experience presupposes consciousness. If we talk of body and mind, whatever the relation that may be asserted, we must really start from two *ideas,* the body-idea and the mind-idea. But ideas are aspects of conscious life: the soul, self or mind is ideas, and these ideas (body, mind) are really only distinctions that arise in consciousness.

This is a hard saying, but in our hearts we admit it is irresistible logic. Perhaps it is more logical than psychological; at least the psychologist generally elects not to face the chances of such a discovery. As our business is psychology we will content ourselves with rehearsing the crucial case in the arguments of Plotinus. Vision is always a topic of great interest. In the days of Plotinus it was progressing among the pupils of Ptolemy who did much to advance the science of optics. But the more we study optics the less we seem to know about the visual experience. We learn enough from science to know that the image on the pupil is not what we look at; we learn enough from medicine to realize the terrible complication of the machinery of vision, with its optic nerve, visual pneuma, and other details. In short the progress of knowledge produces its own collapse; we really only know vision by the actual experience of seeing; it is a part of this experience to eject or project the visual object; experience can never really be anywhere at all, because it is not spatial; it has no extension and cannot be carried in from the outside even in the form of atoms; the real problem is to explain how the experience appears to be in some sense "outer experience." [26]

There are many interesting details in the *Enneads* of Plotinus, but it is most important first to grasp the all-comprehensive nature of this programme; the details follow logically. After Plotinus the major writers accept the new doctrine, most notably Augustine. The religious schools gave it a sympathetic hearing (with some exceptions) because it restated their fundamental beliefs such as "the kingdom of heaven is within you" and "truth dwelleth in the inward parts." The trend of the new doctrine was toward concentration, contemplation, and ecstasy. At first these terms meant definite psychological states, the emphasis falling on attention and interest. Plotinus did for the mind what the physiologists were doing for the body; he discovered the significance of integration. Disintegration or dissipation is bad; integration and concentration are good. Profound interest is abstraction; only the "absent-minded " man is ever truly present with his own mind; for him is reserved the last state of absorption, a complete annihilation of all distraction, when the eyes no longer wander, the ears no longer hear, every sense is quiet and that state is reached which has no name because it is never an object; it is the last union of the self with itself.

V. THE GREAT TRADITION

THE work of Augustine was the last and ripest fruit of antiquity. The scientific progress had already ceased. Galen's industry had collected all the opinions of doctors and philosophers about the nature of man; for twelve hundred years his works were to remain the undisputed authority in that field. The great experiment in politics called the Roman Empire came to an end in A.D. 430. Augustine lived to see the pagan kingdom depart but not to see the City of God take its place. The star of empire now moved eastward and the real centre of political and intellectual activity was at the capital of the Arab empire. While Europe passed through its darkest hour and was a prey to political and economic disorders, the new faith of Islam planted its banners in the ancient kingdom of Persia. In the valley of the Euphrates the victorious Arabs touched the borders of the civilization that had grown old while they still dwelt in tents and sojourned in the wilderness. The

Syrian Christians told the newcomers about the great days of Athens and the wisdom of Hippocrates, Plato, Aristotle, and Galen. The Syrians also talked about the *New Testament,* but the Arabs had their own prophet and were not interested; what they needed was the science, the knowledge of the world and of man, which now seemed to be the gold hidden in this newly discovered mine. Whatever the Arabs lacked, they had curiosity in abundance. The wealth of the conquerors was poured out to obtain translators, to make the wisdom of the Greeks available and to build up the great university of Baghdad. Prices were high and the industry flourished; accuracy was not an essential at this stage; for if the translator did not know much, no one else knew enough to expose his errors. Strange names and figures now wander across the scene. Plato and Aristotle are as much like themselves as their names are like Aflatun and Aristu; but the more we learn of this great movement the more certain it is that the Arabs played a large part in handing on the great tradition from the seventh to the twelfth century.[27]

Though the performance of the Arabs was the most spectacular effort of the period it was

not the only form in which intellectual life continued. The desolation of Europe drove the
peaceful monks westward and made Ireland
during the seventh century a home of learning
and perhaps the only place where Greek survived west of the Danube. From the west came
Eriugena in the ninth century to begin the first
revival of learning. Further research may also
show that the Mediterranean route carried
learning as well as merchandise or crusaders.
The part of Italy which once rejoiced to be
called "Magna Graecia" was perhaps never
quite devoid of Greek elements; Sicily may
have kept some dim memory of the medical
school to which Empedocles belonged and
Greek scholars may have wandered up the roads
that lead to Salerno and Monte Cassino. These
are guesses at truth; the only evidence at present
is the fact that Frederick the Second obviously
considered Sicily to be more progressive than
papal Rome, that this was due in part to Sara-
cens and infidels, and that in the mixed popu-
lation of the Mediterranean border along the old
Phenician route from Palestine to Marseilles
there may have been Greek scholars as compe-
tent as those who stayed in Constantinople.
The movements in the twelfth century are ob-

scure. In the thirteenth century the scene shifts to Spain. The Arab empire creeps along the coast of North Africa and spreads northward to Spain. In this precarious outpost the glory of Baghdad is reproduced for a time; Arab and Jew and Christian meet on the common ground of secular learning; the schools of translators spring up at Cordova and Toledo and with increasing competition the level of work tends to rise; Plato and Aristotle return to Europe after a long journey through Asia Minor, Persia, the north of Egypt, Numidia, and Mauretania. While Spain was beginning to be a centre of learning, Constantinople was reached by the Crusaders going east; and in 1204 some new material was probably acquired. The political empire of the Arabs was already in decline, but their spiritual triumph was complete. Avicenna and Averrhoes were the dominant figures, the great leaders who must be supported or refuted according to the tastes of the individual. Men from all parts eagerly sought to learn from the Arabs what proved, when acquired, to be the lost wisdom of the Greeks.

History explains the peculiar qualities of the thirteenth century. The persistent doctrines of

the Christian church, the great treasury of
Latin thought embalmed in the patristic writings, now became united with the accumulated
knowledge of the world, the physical and physiological sciences created by the Greeks. So
far as concerned the functions of the body and
the natural soul there was no rival to this recovered mass of information. The great teachers of the thirteenth century therefore devoted
their energy to the collection and assimilation
of the new material. The great defect of ancient science was the habit of stating conclusions without recording processes; consequently
there was no real insight into Greek methods
during this period and the recorded knowledge
was accepted as though it had been revealed to
Plato and Aristotle without observation or reasoning on their part. But in spite of that defect the eternal freshness of Greek thinking,
the unprejudiced give and take of the Platonic
dialogues, the appeal of Aristotle to a reason
that was calculative and human, not pure and
transcendental, all these qualities slowly but
surely produced a new attitude toward the
world of natural science.

If we accept the dictum that Plato was never
a Platonist we may add that in the same sense

Aristotle was never an Aristotelian. It is hardly necessary now to argue the point that the reaction against Aristotelianism from Roger Bacon to Francis Bacon was in essence the discovery of the true Aristotle. In some ways Aristotle was not a help; in mechanics or astronomy Archimedes or Aristarchus of Samos were better guides. But in the sciences of human nature, in psychology and politics, the works of Plato and Aristotle were still without a superior. In the sphere of politics the Augustinian tradition was adverse; but the movement toward republicanism originated by Occam and the later movement called Protestantism were both inevitably favourable to arguments that began from the natural endowment of man; in other words, when authority declined, the argument for obligation and political obedience was necessarily based on psychology. In this respect Machiavelli and Melanchthon were united in the same endeavour. Machiavelli derived his ideas of human nature from the classical historians; he learned from the same source that success comes from individual effort and effort is the outcome of desire. As Francis Bacon says, Machiavelli first began to tell us what men are, not what they ought to be. For better or for worse, the whole of the first movement in the new politics was to be dominated by this standpoint; the state is nothing more or less than an equilibrium of forces, a conflict of desires tempered by the calculations of the " cool hour." So Machiavelli laid the egg and Hobbes hatched it. In the effort to show that his political theory was grounded in nature, since nature had then taken the place of divine reason, Hobbes elaborated the psychological theory which justified the political deductions. Thus he became incidentally one of the fathers of modern psychology. To the initiated reader this description will seem hardly correct. For Hobbes had already made his translation of Aristotle's *Rhetoric,* and the most famous phrases in the *Leviathan* are copied literally from the translation. The entire plan is undiluted Aristotle, and for that very reason could be used against the " Aristotelians." The non-classical elements, such as "visible species," are rejected; but in the place of these species we have motion; all sensations are modes of motion, the original doctrine of Aristotle; imagination is a decaying sense, the exact translation of Aristotle's words (v. p. 43); memory is a matter of traces facilitating later motions; reasoning is literally

[145]

syllogismos (συλλογισμός), casting up the accounts. Even more perfect is the summary of the emotional or affective life. Here we have all the details of Aristotle's *Ethics* neatly epitomized. The beginning is made with desire and aversion, movements to and from the object; appetite is the primitive natural tendency to seek satisfaction; wish and deliberation are factors in the higher voluntary movements; finally will is "the last appetite," the deliberative choice of the *Nicomachean Ethics*. Thus modern psychology as understood in the seventeenth century started out fully equipped with a sturdy English version of Aristotle; motion, association of ideas, ratiocination, conation, and volition — all complete. The moralists might object that psychological hedonism was all wrong; the answer was that right and wrong are matters for the reformer, the scientific man must take his facts first and discuss his values later. It was not only in appreciation of the Greek analytic psychology that Hobbes led the way; he also dictated the tone of modern psychology which feels no call to subordinate the facts, or supposed facts, to the prejudices of moralists.

Melanchthon is interesting and important

for other reasons. His position is interesting because in common with all the early reformers he would have preferred to reject Aristotle as part of the Papist heresy. But mere reaction was not a good basis for educating the coming race; it was necessary to look for a master of method, a source from which to draw discipline for the young. The choice fell on Aristotle and Melanchthon pronounced the final judgment in the words: " we cannot do without the monuments of Aristotle." The psychological doctrine was presented in due course in the *Commentarius de Anima,* printed in 1540 for the first time and frequently afterwards at intervals. Melanchthon is important as an educator; whatever we think of his doctrine we must not forget that his works remained standard textbooks for nearly two hundred years, and inevitably affected the mental growth of Europe right through the critical period of transition from mediaeval Catholicism to the new Protestantism.[28]

Though it is possible to trace the language of Hobbes back to Machiavelli in one part and to John of Salisbury in another, it remains practically true that Hobbes formulated the empirical or at least positivistic psychology which was to dominate the eighteenth century. Locke, in spite of some gibes at Aristotelians, produced no psychology that could not be regarded as traditional. His plain method is a return to introspective analysis; it echoes the " clean slate " of antiquity; it requires the traditional machinery of impressions and composition of ideas; it employs the twofold division of sensation and reason, concealing the origin of the latter under the term reflection. Hume was also a faithful adherent of the ancient doctrines. He rejects the faculties of the later doctrines and appears to clean the slate for a fresh start; but in the end he has decided to work with two factors, habit and association. The laws of association given by Hume were apparently taken verbatim from Thomas Aquinas; for Hume had a copy of the *De Anima* of Aquinas, substantially the same as Aristotle's *De Anima*, and was able accordingly to employ the original principles of contiguity and similarity; the addition of causation as a principle of association was an addition to the Greek version but not an ornament. Aristotle was certainly not well known to the philosophers of the eighteenth century; he was an object of suspicion, laughed at by scientific men, and therefore viewed askance by philosophers who thought their salvation lay in reflecting so far as possible the "never enough to be admired Mr. Newton." So long as the mechanistic age was in vogue the Aristotelian views could not be developed. Aristotle was not to be compared with Galileo; and Democritus, who might be lauded as the moving spirit of the seventeenth century, was deplorably lacking in material that could be made into a psychological theory. The result is a perpetual attempt to correlate the Platonic-Aristotelian distinctions of sense, memory, and reason with some form of mechanical dynamics. When at last the study of life and growth gained influence and modern biology showed its first fruits, there was a stronger tendency to know and appreciate the Greek views, both Platonic and Aristotelian.

The biological movement in the sciences is equivalent to the romantic movement in literature. They have a common ground in preferring to study development rather than composition. While the earlier schools discussed the composition and decomposition of the mind, the new movement after 1770 discussed growth and development. This was nearer the Greek methods and in time led to greater appreciation of the heritage of Greek tradition.

In the historical development of Western thought Aristotle was usually regarded as having favoured psychological empiricism. This view was not supported by the text, but since Aristotle supplied so much material on the origin and nature of percepts and sense-functions the error was natural. Plato seemed the very antithesis of this position, because the readers were unable either to read or to understand the more strictly scientific part of Platonism. When the empirical schools of the eigthteenth century showed exactly how much and how little could be achieved by decomposing the mind, there was a tendency to revive Platonism. The mystics were always more or less Platonic; mediaeval Platonism handed on to modern times the one indispensable principle that every fragment of knowledge, though it may be conditioned by the sense, involves a spontaneous act of the soul. Platonism thus became the natural creed of all who believed that consciousness cannot be reduced to physiological terms. This was one of the effects produced by Neo-Platonism. The doctrine persisted through the schools of mysticism down to the seventeenth century. It then appeared as the programme of the Cambridge Platonists who were united in their opposition to sense-empiricism. As the school of the Victorines had insisted on the primacy of "pure" reason, so the Cambridge Platonists took up the defence of mental "acts" against the more extreme theory of "contents" implied in Locke's work. This Platonic theme was worth supporting but it suffered from lack of novelty. Also it invariably led to controversy on points of pure dialectic, especially the case for immortality. Platonic psychology of this kind could yield inspiration perennially but it did not harmonize with the ideals of an age eager to acquire useful knowledge.

Another type of Platonism was developed by the supporters of independent ethical instincts. Shaftesbury and the small number who followed him were representatives of the classical tradition. Against the utilitarian trend of their day they championed the idea of the good as an idea which is moral because it is aesthetic. Their psychology was essentially that which is implied in the phrase "the good and the beautiful." As defending the *feeling* for the beauty of order, not a mediated calculation of benefits, this was a distinct attempt to establish again the Platonic view; it asserted the power of the mind to attain a knowledge of the good transcending the sphere of objects which appeal to the senses. This was the first movement toward the doctrine shortly afterwards expounded by Rousseau. This time the attack on empiricism is conducted in the interests of education. The comparison of Rousseau with Plato is so common a theme that it does not need to be elaborated here. The main point is the very striking way in which Rousseau turns his back on the piece-meal and rote learning of his day. Teaching is to be once more a " turning about of the soul." Children are to learn by contact with nature, by actual mental growth in the solution of their problems; they will find learning a very superior form of play. From Rousseau to the present day there has been a steady stream of educators who sought to rival the Greeks by employing all the arts, music, and dancing to develop a general mental attitude.

Though traditional psychology, not radically different from Aristotle's, persisted to the close of the eighteenth century, it is difficult to say how far the authors were conscious of the fact. Historians of philosophy point out that Aris-

totle's " vitalism " was destroyed by Descartes;
for Descartes surrendered the "vegetative
soul " to physiology, and physiology to mechanics. But this is an insignificant point. Aristotle's " vitalism " never rose above the level
of the biological categories; the body was not
ruled by a mysterious indwelling force, but it
had by virtue of its organic nature a mode of
action which no mere machine possesses. So
long as the Aristotelian classification was kept
and the analysis of the mind was stated in his
terms, the tradition may be regarded as unbroken. How continuous it had been was
shown by Sir William Hamilton. Equipped
with a mass of learning unequalled in his day
(1850) Hamilton could annotate Reid, or any
other writer of that class, by the simple method
of tracing each central idea back to its source;
usually the source was Greek. Even the phrase
" common sense " proved on examination to
be the lineal descendant of Aristotle's " common " or general sensibility through the Latin
translation of the Greek term.

Another important writer of that time who
did much to give Aristotle his due was Jo-
hannes Mueller.[29] The first physiologist in
Europe, he was interested in the problems of

psychology, especially the nature of visual phenomena. The Newtonian optics were not a
contribution to the study of subjective phenomena. Aristotle, Leonardo da Vinci, and
Goethe were almost the only important names
that could be quoted in the field of colour
phenomena as experiences. While Mueller's
work shows the way in which Aristotle as a
scientific observer commanded respect in those
days, the credit of presenting an Aristotle that
justified so much respect must go to Zeller. In
spite of its defects, Zeller's *Philosophy of the
Greeks* must always remain the most conspicuous example of the great revival which
followed Hegel's cosmic outlines. Since those
days histories of philosophy have been ever
more abounding, but the achievement of Zeller
remains the monument which marks the new
era of understanding, the more complete knowledge of what the Greeks really thought and
said.

At this climax we may fittingly close the
record. When the Greeks receive their due it
must be rendered in monuments and histories.
Nobody endowed with the practical sense which
the Greeks loved or properly inspired by the
doctrine of the mean, will attempt to argue that

ancient psychology has not been surpassed and abandoned. In art and religion there are qualities which seem truly timeless; the history of art or of religion is not cumulative; there is no increment of years which can be added to Sophocles to make him a Shakespeare. But all knowledge of fact, all scientific knowledge is cumulative. For that reason the modern achievement so far surpasses the ancient that comparison becomes futile. On the other side of the account we may reckon the fact that a building which adds section upon section through two thousand years and yet presents astonishing continuity and stability, must have been founded on a firm basis. That was the great merit of the Greeks who laid the foundation, and it deserves to be commemorated " with natural piety." Still more might be said to support the plea that in many respects the Greek point of view has never been fully understood or quite superseded, but that might develop into special pleading and would certainly obscure the distinction between philosophy and psychology which now dominates our departmentalized institutions of learning. As the Greeks made no such distinction it is a delicate task to observe conscientiously the lines of cleavage. In this comparatively brief account of our debt to the Greeks and Romans in the sphere of psychology, the material has been chosen, carefully, so that the contents of the book might be true to its title.

NOTES AND BIBLIOGRAPHY

NOTES

1. P. 17. For further details see *The Evolution of Anatomy*, Charles Singer, London, 1925.

2. P. 20. This statement might be disputed. Some scholars and historians consider that some nerves, e.g. the optic nerves were known earlier. In any case little use was made of the knowledge and the terms are vague. The idea of a nervous system is not earlier than the Alexandrian school.

3. P. 28. A good general account of this subject is given by Clifford Allbutt, *Greek Medicine in Rome*, London, 1921, p. 224, " Pneumatism."

4. P. 32. " We do not see with the eyes; rather we see through them. . . . It would surely be strange if we had placed within us, like so many warriors in Trojan horses, a multitude of sensory faculties which did not tend to unite in some form, call it soul or some other name etc.," *Theaet.*, 184D, quoted Beare 261 (see Bibliography).

5. P. 36. See *Anal. Post.*, ii. 19, or *De An.*, 428a: though the translators often use " judge " to convey the meaning, Aristotle's term implies the more profound fact that discrimination, e.g. of colours, is correlative with sense-development.

6. P. 39. *E. N.*, iii. 10 (1118a).

7. P. 41. See *De An.*, 424a18, for this definition; also 415b24 for definition of sensation as qualitative change.

8. P. 43. The phrase " decaying sense " is due to Hobbes who was translating Aristotle's *Rhetoric*, 1370a28.

9. P. 44. See *Post. Analytics*, 100a12.

10. P. 47. See Hammond, *Aristotle's Psychology*, p. 195, for translation of this remarkable treatise.

11. P. 50. See especially *De An.*, 428-9. The quotation below is from Hammond, p. 205 = *De Mem.*, ii.

12. P. 54. Aristotle, *De Insomn.*, ii. quoted from Hammond, p. 236.

13. P. 54. Aristotle says it is impossible to think without a "phantasm," *De Mem.*, 449b31. It is interesting to find a definite opinion about "imageless thinking" so early in the history of psychology.

14. P. 59. *Republic*, iv. 439.

15. P. 66. This doctrine of appetite and will is summarized in *Nicomachean Ethics*, Bk. iii. 1–4. It is reproduced in Hobbes, *Leviathan*, Bk. i., Chapt. 6.

16. P. 67. See *E. N.*, ii. 1.

17. P. 69. See this summary given in *Politics*, vii. 13 (1332).

18. P. 72. See *E. N.*, vii. An interesting discussion of Aristotle's analysis will be found in "Psychology and Psychical Research" by T. W. Mitchell, pp. 151–5, in Wm. Brown's *Psychology and the Sciences*, London, 1924. As that writer points out we really have no equivalent for the Greek word 'ακρασία, (*akrasia*) and it would be better to keep it as a technical term for this kind of mental disintegration.

19. P. 80. For the meaning of imitation see *Republic*, Bk. iii. 401, from which the passage below is quoted.

20. P. 85. Adam Smith, *Moral Sentiments*, Part i, Sect. i. "When we see a stroke aimed and just ready to fall upon the leg or arm of another person, we naturally shrink and draw back our own leg or our own arm . . . the mob, when they are gazing at a dancer on the slack rope, naturally writhe and twist and balance their own bodies as they see him do etc." For Smith and Tarde see Brett, *History of Psychology*, Vol. ii. p. 356 and Vol. iii. p. 289.

21. P. 93. See *Republic*, vi–vii. 509–521.

22. P. 106. *Laws*, Bk. v. 734.

23. P. 111. *Republic*, ix. 571.

24. P. 120. See *De Motu Animalium*, 701b (Oxford translation and Notes).

25. P. 130. Quintilian: see *De Oratore*, ii. 86.

26. P. 137. The theory of vision in Plotinus is well

stated by T. Whittaker, *The Neo-Platonists*, Cambridge, 1918. The resemblance to Berkeley's *Theory of Vision* is obvious.

27. P. 140. Details of the transmission of doctrine are given in Brett, *History of Psychology*, Vol. ii.

28. P. 147. On the subject of Protestant doctrines in relation to Aristotle see P. Petersen, *Geschichte der Aristotelischen Philosophie im Protestantischen Deutschland*, Leipzig, 1921.

29. P. 153. On Mueller's work see G. H. Lewes, *Aristotle*, London, 1864, p. 228. Goethe wrote a *Geschichte der Farbenlehre* which helped to arouse interest in the subject and in 1849 Karl von Prantl wrote a work called *Aristoteles ueber die Farben*, München.

BIBLIOGRAPHY

A. Sources.

Bailey, Cyril, *Epicurus:* the extant remains with short critical apparatus; translation and notes. Oxford, 1926.

Bréhier, Émile, *Plotin, Ennéades.* 2 vols. Paris, 1924. (text and translations in the *Budé* Series)

Burnet, John, *Early Greek Philosophy.*[2] London, 1908.

Diels, Hermann, *Die Fragmente der Vorsokratiker;* Griechisch u. deutsch.[2] Berlin, 1906–1910.

Hammond, W. A., *Aristotle's Psychology: De Anima* and *Parva Naturalia,* translated. London, 1902.

Hicks, R. D., *Aristoteles, De Anima,* text, with commentary and translation. Cambridge, 1907.

Kühn, C. G., *Galeni Opera Omnia.* Lipsiae, 1821–1833. (cf. Brock, Arthur John, *Galen on the Natural Faculties,* with an English Translation, in *The Loeb Classical Library,* London and New York, 1916)

Moser, G. H., and Creuzer, F., *Plotini Opera Omnia.* 3 vols. Oxonii, 1835.

Pearson, A. C., *The Fragments of Zeno and Cleanthes.* London, 1891.

Ross, W. D., and Smith, J. A., (Editors) *The Works of Aristotle,* Oxford Translations of Aristotle. Oxford, in progress.

Stratton, G. M., *Theophrastus, De Sensibus;* text and translation. London, 1917.

Usener, Hermann, *Epicurea.* Lipsiae, 1887. (anastatic reprint, 1903)

Von Arnim, J., *Stoicorum Veterum Fragmenta.* 3 vols. Leipzig, 1903–1924.

[also, texts of Plato: *The Republic, Timaeus, Philebus, Symposium;* editions, e.g., Adam, J., *The Republic,* 2 vols., Cambridge, England, 1902; translations, e.g., of Jowett,

[162]

BIBLIOGRAPHY

Benjamin, 4 vols., Oxford, 1871; and Hort, Sir Arthur, *Theophrastus' Enquiry into Plants,* with an English translation, in *The Loeb Classical Library,* 2 vols., New York and London, 1916; Ogle, William, *De Partibus Animalium,* English Translation, Oxford, 1911; Platt, Arthur, *De Generatione Animalium,* English Translation, Oxford, 1910; Thompson, D'Arcy Wentworth, *Historia Animalium,* English Translation, Oxford, 1910.]

B. REFERENCES.

The material for an account of ancient psychology has, for the most part, to be selected from books of which only special parts are concerned with psychological questions. It is, therefore, difficult to give references which are exactly or exclusively concerned with psychology. The following titles represent works which are especially worth consulting:

BEARE, J. I., *Greek Theories of Elementary Cognition from Alcmaeon to Aristotle.* Oxford, 1906.

BRETT, GEORGE S., *History of Psychology, Ancient and Patristic.* London, 1912.

CHAIGNET, A. ÉDOUARD, *Histoire de la Psychologie des Grecs,* 5 vols. Paris, 1887–1893. *Essai sur la Psychologie d'Aristote.* Paris, 1883.

CHAUVET, EMMANUEL, *La Philosophie des Médecins Grecs.* Paris, 1886.

HICKS, R. D., *Stoic and Epicurean.* New York, 1910.

ROHDE, ERWIN, *Psyche,* Seelenkult und Unsterblichkeitsglaube der Griechen.[2] Freiburg, 1898. (translation, *Psyche,* the Cult of Souls and Belief in Immortality among the Greeks, London and New York, 1925, in " The International Library of Psychology, Philosophy and Scientific Method ")

ROSS, W. D., *Aristotle.* New York, 1924. (c.v. " Psychology ")

SIEBECK, H., *Geschichte der Psychologie.* Gotha, 1880–1884.

STEIN, L., *Die Erkenntnisstheorie der Stoa.* Berlin, 1888.

BIBLIOGRAPHY

C. As psychology is part of the science of organisms, the reader should have some acquaintance with the general background. For this purpose, the following works may be consulted:

ALLBUTT, SIR THOMAS CLIFFORD, *Greek Medicine in Rome*. London, 1921.

SINGER, CHARLES, (1) " Biology " and " Medicine," pp. 163–248, in *The Legacy of Greece* (edited by R. W. Livingstone). Oxford, 1922.

——, (2) *Greek Biology and Greek Medicine*. Oxford, 1920. (The World's Manuals)

STOCKS, J. L., *Aristotelianism*. New York and London, 1925. (in the *Our Debt to Greece and Rome* Series)

TAYLOR, A. E., (1) *Platonism and Its Influence*. New York and London, 1924. (in the *Our Debt to Greece and Rome* Series)

——, (2) *Plato, The Man and his Work*. London, 1926.

TAYLOR, H. O., *Greek Biology and Medicine*. New York and London, 1922. (in the *Our Debt to Greece and Rome* Series)

Our Debt to Greece and Rome

AUTHORS AND TITLES

HOMER. *John A. Scott.*

SAPPHO. *David M. Robinson.*

EURIPIDES. *F. L. Lucas.*

ARISTOPHANES. *Louis E. Lord.*

DEMOSTHENES. *Charles D. Adams.*

THE POETICS OF ARISTOTLE. *Lane Cooper.*

GREEK RHETORIC AND LITERARY CRITICISM. *W. Rhys Roberts.*

LUCIAN. *Francis G. Allinson.*

CICERO AND HIS INFLUENCE. *John C. Rolfe.*

CATULLUS. *Karl P. Harrington.*

LUCRETIUS AND HIS INFLUENCE. *George Depue Hadzsits.*

OVID. *Edward Kennard Rand.*

HORACE. *Grant Showerman.*

VIRGIL. *John William Mackail.*

SENECA THE PHILOSOPHER. *Richard Mott Gummere.*

APULEIUS. *Elizabeth Hazelton Haight.*

MARTIAL. *Paul Nixon.*

PLATONISM. *Alfred Edward Taylor.*

ARISTOTELIANISM. *John L. Stocks.*

STOICISM. *Robert Mark Wenley.*

LANGUAGE AND PHILOLOGY. *Roland G. Kent.*

AUTHORS AND TITLES

AESCHYLUS AND SOPHOCLES. *J. T. Sheppard.*

GREEK RELIGION. *Walter Woodburn Hyde.*

SURVIVALS OF ROMAN RELIGION. *Gordon J. Laing.*

MYTHOLOGY. *Jane Ellen Harrison.*

ANCIENT BELIEFS IN THE IMMORTALITY OF THE SOUL. *Clifford H. Moore.*

STAGE ANTIQUITIES. *James Turney Allen.*

PLAUTUS AND TERENCE. *Gilbert Norwood.*

ROMAN POLITICS. *Frank Frost Abbott.*

PSYCHOLOGY, ANCIENT AND MODERN. *G. S. Brett.*

ANCIENT AND MODERN ROME. *Rodolfo Lanciani.*

WARFARE BY LAND AND SEA. *Eugene S. Mc-Cartney.*

THE GREEK FATHERS. *James Marshall Campbell.*

GREEK BIOLOGY AND MEDICINE. *Henry Osborn Taylor.*

MATHEMATICS. *David Eugene Smith.*

LOVE OF NATURE AMONG THE GREEKS AND ROMANS. *H. R. Fairclough.*

ANCIENT WRITING AND ITS INFLUENCE. *B. L. Ullman.*

GREEK ART. *Arthur Fairbanks.*

ARCHITECTURE. *Alfred M. Brooks.*

ENGINEERING. *Alexander P. Gest.*

MODERN TRAITS IN OLD GREEK LIFE. *Charles Burton Gulick.*

ROMAN PRIVATE LIFE. *Walton Brooks McDaniel.*

GREEK AND ROMAN FOLKLORE. *William Reginald Halliday.*

ANCIENT EDUCATION. *J. F. Dobson.*